HACKING
STUDENT LEARNING
HABITS

9 **WAYS** TO
FOSTER RESILIENT
LEARNERS AND **ASSESS**
THE **PROCESS,**
NOT THE **OUTCOME**

HACK™
Learning
SERIES

ELIZABETH
JORGENSEN

TIMES
TEN

Highland Heights, OH
10publications.com

Mark Barnes, Publisher; Joy Scott Ressler, Associate Publisher; Jennifer Jas, Senior Editor; Jennifer Marshall, Developmental Editor; Steven Plummer, Designer.

All web links in this book are correct as of the publication date below but may have become inactive or otherwise modified since that time.

PAPERBACK ISBN: 978-1-956512-15-1
E-BOOK ISBN: 978-1-956512-16-8
HARDCOVER ISBN: 978-1-956512-17-5

Library of Congress Cataloging-in-Publication Data is available for this title.
First Printing: April 2022

To Nancy Jorgensen, my mother and most influential teacher.

TABLE OF CONTENTS

IMPLEMENT PROCESS-BASED ASSESSMENT

Trust the process. Your time is coming. Just do the work, and the results will handle themselves.
— Tony Gaskins, motivational speaker

M Y COLLEAGUES AND I gathered around a lunch table as the students walked out of the cafeteria, backpacks slung over their shoulders, laptops tucked under their arms.

"This is my dream job," I said. It was a Wisconsin late-summer evening, and our school's college essay workshop had just ended. "How can we get this to happen in the fall in our classrooms?" I wanted to carry over the eagerness our workshop students displayed. "How can we get kids to try things out, to commit to learning and growing?"

The college essay workshop felt like a utopian experience, with three teachers collaborating to instruct eager and invested students. For four days, eighty-some college-bound seniors sat in front of us. Although some were there because their parents required it, most arrived of their own volition. Although each could have left at any time, they stayed. And they did more than stay; they brought us draft after draft. They analyzed structure. They questioned punctuation choices. They mulled over topics. They discussed goals. They asked about the effectiveness of specific paragraphs and full sections. The students took risks, telling emotional and powerful stories. They used innovation and creativity. During the college essay workshop, the students dedicated themselves to writing the best sentences, transitions, hooks, and conclusions they could. They listened to their classmates and to us, and they applied feedback in meaningful ways.

"I think we can," my colleague said. "But we need students to care about their daily work as much as they care about their college essays."

A decade ago, my writing colleagues and I started offering college essay workshops. They're a collaborative, gradeless endeavor. Students earn a quarter credit if they come all four days, but the students don't care about the quarter credit. They care about writing good essays, getting into dream schools, earning scholarships, and receiving grants.

I wondered out loud, "Do letter grades squelch progress? Or do students simply need an authentic purpose?"

In the years when college essays were vital to admissions, students in the college essay workshop came in with questions, excited to create and submit applications. They identified their weaknesses and saw us as their partners and teammates, as their loudest advocates and cheerleaders. The students had a purpose for their work and goals they wanted to achieve. Students knew there was no one right way to attack the prompt or compose the essay.

My colleagues and I tabled the discussion, promising to research ways to create this atmosphere in our traditional classrooms.

In our writing classes, we had already abandoned rubrics. We found they stifled creativity, prevented risk-taking, and provided a blueprint for blandness. But even without a rubric, we struggled to get kids to commit to their writing, to fully embrace risks, and to follow their passions.

And, without a rubric, I questioned my grading policies. Was I fairly and accurately assessing? I often felt guilty about giving an A, B, or C on an essay about a dying father, a poem about anorexia, a limerick about mental health, or a narrative about self-doubt.

Since college essay workshop students flourished in a no-grade environment, was this the answer to motivating students in regular classrooms?

As my colleagues and I explored the ways other teachers built classroom cultures rich in creativity and productivity and assessed their students' progress, we found our state's Department of Public Instruction offered a summit. Teams of teachers could apply to attend the weekend-long exploration.

THE TEXT OF OUR STATE SUMMIT APPLICATION:

We offer a summer college essay writing workshop that's authentic and gradeless. Seeking to replicate this experience, we've searched for how to transfer these concepts to our classrooms. In teaching writing, students remain resistant to drafting and revising essays. They focus, instead, on rubrics and how to earn a grade, not on how to write well. As teachers, we've witnessed that rubrics do little to encourage student growth. Although a rubric expedites grading, it's not a successful learning tool. Eliminating grades and rubrics, we will encourage and develop student writers to achieve their potential. We hope this summit will allow us to flesh out details, logistics, and research on how to better meet the needs of students. We shared our idea with our department chair, and he was enthusiastic and approved.

Image 0.1

My college essay workshop colleagues and I applied to the summit (see Image 0.1). We were accepted and attended, eager to engineer an innovative plan.

At the summit, our team worked with a facilitator; she asked us questions, led us through a logic model, and played devil's advocate. With her help, we realized grades failed to motivate or improve writing; we learned that if we instead fostered a dynamic, stimulating, compelling, and vigorous process, our students would be more willing to embrace writing, to take risks, to commit to their words, to care, and to be works in progress.

At the conference, we fleshed out our plan to inspire students to invest, set goals, follow their passions, learn about themselves and their talents, put in daily work, take chances, and experiment. We discussed how to encourage students to really dive in and understand that each part of the process is important, to embrace each assignment as a challenge or opportunity, and to focus not on the grade but on the process.

● ● ●

Process-based assessment helps students build learning habits as they:

- practice skills
- reframe comparison to identify what led to an outcome
- develop a growth mindset
- improve based on feedback
- continue to move forward
- accept imperfection
- enjoy learning and improving

Process-based assessment helps teachers to:

- focus on skill-building rather than grading
- provide guidance and support for students
- work collaboratively with students to develop lifelong, high-yielding habits

● ● ●

In *Atomic Habits*, James Clear writes about Professor Uelsmann, who divided his students into two groups of photographers. One group, which he named the quantity group, was assessed based on the number of photos captured. The other group, called the quality group, was assessed based on the quality of one image.

Throughout the semester, the quantity group played with composition, lighting, and point of view. Students in the quantity group took photos outside and inside. They used multiple lenses and different equipment. They experimented with angles and subjects and tested theories. They shared their body of work and sought out, listened to, and applied feedback. They made mistakes and learned from them.

PROCESS-BASED ASSESSMENT CAN BE USED IN EVERY GRADE, IN EVERY SUBJECT.

In contrast, the quality group thought about what would create a perfect picture. These students didn't go through the process of taking photos. They didn't test or experiment. Instead, they hypothesized and pondered. And then, they attempted one perfect image.

At the end of the semester, Professor Uelsmann found that all the best photographs came from the quantity group. The students in that group tried, failed, learned, and grew. They developed skills and made progress through a process of trial and error. In contrast, the quality group found themselves paralyzed by the pursuit of one perfect image.

Similarly, many of our students get stuck on the idea of perfection. They believe an A-plus on a paper or test will provide happiness or indicate future success. They think a thirty-six on the ACT will lead to their dream school, which will lead to their dream job and their dream life. They think one perfect photograph exists. And then, they refuse to try to capture it because they're convinced they'll fail.

By removing outcome-based grades and assessing the process, we break our students from this mindset.

● ● ●

Process-based assessment can be used in every grade, in every subject. Start by asking three questions:

1. **Why do I value the process?** Your "why" is your purpose. By knowing why, you'll be better able to answer questions two and three.

2. **What are students expected to accomplish?** Choose goals that are measurable and attainable.

3. **How can my classroom center around the process?** Identify behaviors or habits that will focus students on learning and growing rather than on earning a grade.

How I answered these questions:

1. I want my students to find pleasure in writing, to know their voices matter, to realize writing can be cathartic, to understand that writing is never done or perfect, to take the skills they develop in class and apply them to their lives, to gain confidence, and to know that work and daily attention to detail allow them to improve.

2. Students will create pieces they are proud of, enjoy writing, approach the work with confidence and an increased understanding of their strengths and weaknesses, and share their voices with the world.

3. The writing process is not linear. It is different for each student and may include brainstorming, drafting, writing, editing, sharing, revising, submitting, and publishing. To focus on the process rather than the outcome, I will present each part of the writing process with equal importance.

● ● ●

Grades and assessment are not synonymous. Grades are ineffective assessments. Process-based assessments, however, allow students to know how far they are from the goal and how to move closer to it.

Grades are an unreliable comparison to a standard, placing students somewhere on the A-to-F scale. Although grades can be part of assessment, assessment is effective because it requires student participation. Assessment relies on a collaborative goal; it encourages conversations and improvements; and it evaluates the process, not the outcome. Do not think of what needs a grade. Instead, consider how assessment can enhance a student's process and assist them in improving.

GRADES ARE POOR QUALITY, INEFFECTIVE ASSESSMENTS. PROCESS-BASED ASSESSMENTS, HOWEVER, ALLOW STUDENTS TO KNOW HOW FAR THEY ARE FROM THE GOAL AND HOW TO MOVE CLOSER TO IT.

● ● ●

At my school, the writing teachers instilled a process-based assessment system that encourages students to value each part of the writing process and to develop excellent, long-lasting learning habits. Process-based assessment moves away from rigid rules and encourages students to learn and grow, gain insight about themselves and their skills, and practice daily habits consistently. Process-based assessment allows students to make small, sustainable changes that lead them to growth.

Daily habits and a process-based environment encourage students to care about improving their processes rather than earning a grade or achieving an outcome.

A process-based classroom enables students to:

- make mistakes

- learn from their mistakes

- do more of what works and less of what doesn't

Because we work within a system that requires grades, students earn points for working through the writing process. A process point can be assigned when a student:

- demonstrates growth

- shows progress

- produces work that requires revision

- attempts a step

Receiving a process point does not mean the assignment is perfect, complete, or A-quality work. Conversely, not receiving a process point is not failure, the end of the world, or detrimental to a student's overall grade. Because the process is cumulative and each step is important, no late work is accepted. Students are expected to attempt all steps on time, to learn from unsuccessful attempts, and to continue successful ones. Process-based assessment holds students accountable for using class time to focus on skill-building. Daily, students:

- receive time and space to experiment

- practice, understanding that production will occasionally suffer

- are assessed on behaviors and habits, not outcomes

In class, students read and analyze model texts and peer examples. They research and write. They draft and edit. They peer edit and share drafts with me. They ask questions, discuss language choices, and try out metaphors and similes. They connect with professional authors. They learn from feedback from friends, family, and peers. Along the way, I pose questions, and I meet students where they are and provide a cheer, reminding them they can and will create beautiful art worthy of sharing. At its core, process-based assessment is about personalized instruction for each student every day to help them create positive learning habits.

Think of a piano student learning a Bach or Chopin piece. It's such a long process. The student starts with one page, and even that is broken down into the left hand and right hand. With practice, the student learns all the notes. Then, they work on speed or getting it up to tempo. Then, they add dynamics, then phrasing. It takes daily work, with many failures, before the piece is ready for performance.

At the beginning of the semester, I outline process-based assessment in a letter for students and explain it in the course syllabus. Students hear me verbally describe what process-based assessment looks like.

Parents also have access to the syllabus and welcome letter and can view the course management system.

Students understand that the writing teachers have set process-based boundaries, and we will stick to them. We will follow through on our promises, and all parts of the process are worth equal value: research, brainstorms, drafts, papers, and peer edits. Even the final exam is worth one process point. See Appendix A to read the letter I provided to students at the beginning of the course.

In addition to hearing from the teacher about process-based assessment and reading about it in the syllabus (see Image 0.2), students also receive a letter from a previous semester's student. See Appendix B to read the letter from a former student to a current student.

CLASS SYLLABUS EXCERPT ABOUT PROCESS-BASED ASSESSMENT:

Standards of Evaluation

- Grades are based upon the work completed *throughout the writing process.*
- Each assignment, experience, task, or day may earn a point.
- There is no rounding of grades.
- No late work is accepted.
- Work must be submitted before the end of the class period.

Grading Rules

Since many class days include writing time, the late policy is rigid. Students should always use the appropriate electronic file and procedure to share work.

Image 0.2

After incorporating process-based assessment in our classes, students said:

> "It is refreshing to see a class focused more on improvement and growth than numbers and scores. It is much easier to flourish in an environment that encourages errors than one where you are too scared to attempt new challenges."

> "The emphasis on progress and development greatly appeals to me because it contrasts with what teachers focused on in the past. Instead of trying to improve the [skills], previous teachers placed all importance on the finished product. While this has improved my grades, my [skills have] not improved."

"As I grew up teachers had very strict guidelines that I had to follow and I stopped enjoying [learning] as much as I had before. I am going to have much more flexibility … than I have in the past and I am excited for that."

My college essay workshop colleagues and I continue to tweak our process-based assessment model. It looks a bit different each year, and we remain open to revising, learning, and growing, just as we ask our students to be. In our journey, we've found there is no magic formula to process-based assessment. We can only do what works with this batch of students. We can only do our best work each day.

As I wrote this book, I interviewed countless teachers and discovered new approaches and strategies. I learned how teachers of every subject and across every grade level use process-based assessment in their classrooms to help students create learning habits. I was inspired by my colleagues, far and near, who have built innovative, process-based classrooms that allow each student to be the best version of themselves, working toward their individual goals each day. I am confident you will too.

CREATE PROCESS-BASED LEARNING HABITS
Support Skill-Building

The goal is not to be perfect by the end.
The goal is to be better today.
— SIMON SINEK, AUTHOR AND INSPIRATIONAL SPEAKER

THE PROBLEM: Students chase outcomes

SCHOOLS ARE DRIVEN by grades. Students aim to earn top marks, while teachers feel bound by systems that require them to circle boxes on rubrics or administer multiple-choice tests.

In a typical grading environment, students flip to the back page of their essay or look to the top of their test. Then, they glance at their classmates and ask, "What did you get?" Some search for a way to boost their self-worth, others seek to commiserate. For most, it's compare-and-despair. Yet, most medical schools don't have grades but pass, fail, and honors.

The problem with grades is that they're easily manipulated and notoriously unreliable because these types of outcomes don't accurately reflect student potential or achievement. What does an ACT score say about what a student can do when they sit in a university lecture hall or attend their first day of boot camp or get their dream internship? Grades are subjective: they may reflect a concept that was arbitrarily included or reviewed, a teacher's mood, a successful guess, or even cheating. Good grades may also lead students to believe they have mastered a concept or found proficiency when all they've done is received a score.

Teachers may use grades punitively when a student doesn't follow directions or play by the rules. A teacher may think they're teaching the student a lesson when they downgrade an assignment, but what they're doing is making students resent school and those who enforce requirements.

Outcome-based environments are a source of stress for both teachers and students. Students, like teachers, are inundated with tools and data, and none of us knows where to start. Teachers are asked to see scores as a set of data points, while students either don't care about the results or overemphasize bragging or boasting. What does the score say about how the student can improve? How does the grade help move the student forward? What does scoring a percentage up or down say about the student's abilities or the teacher's success? The problem is that grades do not help students focus on learning or growing.

Grades aren't the only data points; teachers also receive student Individualized Education Plans or notes from case managers. Administrative software lights up student names in color codes, alerting us to Lexile scores, standardized test results, and interventions. Especially early in the semester, this information is suffocating. We don't yet know our students, so we cannot begin to associate the data with the faces in our classrooms. And then, when it comes time to report end-of-the-year results, data can easily be manipulated to prove progress.

What does this all mean for teachers and students? Standards-based grades have created an environment of competition and outcomes. But students are not to blame for chasing outcomes. They've been placed in an incentive-based, outcome-driven system. Whether it's aiming for a test score, an ACT mark, or acceptance into an Ivy League school, students focus on an end result that is often uncontrollable and unachievable rather than on the processes that could lead them to do their best.

THE HACK: Create process-based learning habits

A process-based classroom encourages a series of habits that lead each student to do their best. It is about embracing, trying, failing, and trying again. To reduce outcome-based thinking, create an environment that focuses on the process: the small controllables that students experience in class each day.

By building constructive daily habits, students increase their likelihood of positive results, not only in your class but in any endeavor. It's about turning the "*What* did you get on the test?" to "*How* did you get that on the test?" It's about helping students develop higher-order thinking skills to become problem-solvers. In changing the question from what to how, students maximize their skills rather than adhere to specific teachers' procedures or regurgitate copies.

We can never know a student's final results, but we can be there to guide them on their explorations. Our students will change their minds a million times, but we can start to predict where they will end up in ten, twenty, or fifty years by looking at the daily habits they're executing. Habits give us a peek into the future, and good habits expand the opportunity for success. Are they reading each day? Are they getting proper sleep and nutrition? It's the small habits that design their future.

Our students are all in different places for different reasons and will move forward at different paces. Help them acknowledge their power to make a change, commit to consistency, and improve their performance via challenging tasks, little by little, one small chunk at a time.

Start by asking your students to do a task for five minutes. Maybe it is trying a math problem, researching a topic, or working with clay. Give students a start and end time to make the task more manageable. Tell them it's okay to quit when the time is up. What students will find, however, is that usually, they won't need or want to stop once they start the task. If they decide to quit, help them try a different task in the next block of minutes.

Each student's process will differ, so encourage them to take a risk and do what only they could do—not to emulate exemplars but to be inspired by them. Provide in-class time each day for students to gather ideas, attempt challenges, collaborate on projects, celebrate small victories, and play.

● ● ●

Terri Carnell teaches writing to juniors and seniors, and she uses ordinary tactics in new ways to engage students. At some point in the semester, Carnell asks her students to write about pet peeves. Students start by reading and discussing an article about pet peeves. She says they often comment on how pet peeves are a contrast to the previous unit on gratitude. She says, "Students realize that pet peeves are not just ranting but about being positive." Carnell then provides students with an example pet peeve essay she wrote. (Read the essay in Appendix C.)

She hopes her model is entertaining. She says, "The least-likely student to engage is usually the one to participate when we talk about pet peeves because they hate the slow driver, or they have road rage, or they can't stand the fork clicking on teeth or how their dad chews."

In addition to pet peeves, Carnell says her students enjoy goofy activities. To encourage creativity, she asks each student to write a random, short sentence on paper. Then, she tells the students to crumple up the paper and chuck it across the room. After throwing the paper, students get up, pick up a random one, and then use that sentence in their writing. Students continue throwing and picking up paper until the time is up.

"Although the stories can be a bit odd, the activity gets students moving and riled up about writing," she says. "When it comes time to share, it's usually the kids who speak the least who get involved."

When Carnell teaches a unit on interviewing, she starts with an exercise to help students practice listening and asking questions. To do this, she sticks a character's name on each student's back. Students ask classmates yes-or-no questions to figure out who they are. By asking closed questions, students learn what questions might be better when they conduct an interview.

She says students are also "practicing looking at someone in the face, communicating, and talking with a variety of people."

Carnell instills daily routines and procedures to cultivate a process-based environment. In your classroom, what can students expect to practice every day? Can they expect to have time to move and to connect with classmates?

Set boundaries, prioritizing what's best for your kids. Build in time for self-care, gratitude, and enjoyment. What do your students enjoy doing? What energizes them? How can you do more of that?

John Warner, known as The Biblioracle, says, "I don't want to improve students' writing. I want to help them be writers. Writing is a practice involving not just skills but knowledge, attitudes, and habits of mind as well. Focusing on 'improvement' can overshadow parts of the practice other than skills." Whether or not you're teaching writing, this concept applies. Focus students on effort instead of results; help them to practice grit and delayed gratification.

HELP STUDENTS OWN THEIR PROCESSES BY ASKING THEM TO IDENTIFY WHEN THEY ARE READY TO MOVE ON TO THE NEXT STEP.

A process-based environment is about taking another step, no matter how small. It's these habits repeated and reinforced in your classroom's environment that build success. It's not about perfect practice—which doesn't exist—but an effort. This helps to focus students on learning instead of grades; it also helps produce the best performances. In your classroom, let go of perfection; instead, welcome setbacks and forget the results. Focus on passion and helping each student improve. See Image 1.1 for ideas of words to share with students to remind them to invest in the process-based learning environment.

WORDS TO SHARE WITH STUDENTS TO REMIND THEM TO INVEST IN THE PROCESS-BASED LEARNING ENVIRONMENT:

- Practice is progress.

- Give me today's best.

- Decide what you want to change and what you want to remain the same.

- You have the power to improve.

- You control your progress through your habits.

Image 1.1

Appealing classrooms help foster a process-based environment. Create stations or seating options. Allow students to choose their group members or to move around the room. When students work on a piece about nature, venture outside to smell, taste, feel, hear, and see. When they express interest in rockets, bring in models they can touch, watch videos of rockets, and encourage students to share their experiences with rockets. Make your classroom a place that fosters wonder and innovation.

Help students own their processes by asking them to identify when they are ready to move on to the next step. While students accumulate little bits of knowledge that build over time, help them find opportunities to use feedback to improve. See Hack 6: Generate Feedback Loops for more details.

Take a cue from the theater department. Actors in the school play use routines to prepare for performances. A deadline states when actors must be off-script and books are no longer allowed onstage. Dress rehearsals provide a simulated experience, with full costume, makeup, musicians, lights, and sound. Before opening night, students perform a practice for elementary schools. On performance nights, a call sheet incorporates deadlines (call time, makeup time, vocal warm-ups, stage call, and curtain speech). In these routines, the director builds and nurtures a successful system.

Be picky about how your students spend time. Block times and prioritize. View your classroom like putting together a puzzle. Don't worry about the whole picture; focus on which piece you need now. Take it one piece at a time.

Each day, provide class time for students to practice. Your classroom's environment offers an escape from the stress or pressure they may be feeling. Your class is a time for students to be mindful and only concentrate on the task(s) at hand. Avoid micromanaging, and instead, allow students space to engage with peers and invest in themselves. Remain flexible and embrace diverse ways to achieve results. Remove arbitrary requirements (like a number of paragraphs), and instead, ask students to wow you with creativity. Maybe students will create a dance, give a demonstration, construct a slide deck, or produce a recording or music video.

● ● ●

Carnell often helps students with college essays in her composition classes and at workshops. One student wrote an essay that explored how she associated a food with a loss in her life. But the student said she no longer loved the essay. She said she felt it didn't show as much about herself as she wanted it to. Carnell asked the student if she had any other ideas. The student said she liked a different prompt about what makes her lose track of time. She also gushed about her favorite book (that she found in fourth grade); a love of reading shared with her great-aunt and great-uncle; and her current read, a book lent to her by the parents of the boy she babysat. Carnell removed roadblocks with dialogue. Talking through ideas and thinking before taking the next step of the writing process helped affirm the student's direction and provided her with the resolve to begin a new draft. When students feel stuck in a process-based environment, Carnell uses the habits of dialogue and reflection to move students forward.

Like Carnell, you can build an environment that normalizes starting over. Help students remove judgment and evaluate their performances as objective, neutral data points. Ask them to identify what works for them because what works for them is what they will continue to do. Knowing what works is equally important to knowing what doesn't. Once students recognize what doesn't work, help them pinpoint weaknesses that sabotage performances. Work with them to remedy or eliminate weaknesses. See Hack 7: Re-Evaluate and Move Forward for tips on building resilience.

Consider the situation when patients see a physical therapist. It's not about doing the exercise perfectly but about putting in the reps. Some patients spend months in the hospital and need to relearn how to walk. Every day, the patient will take a few steps. They will use a walker, then a cane. When they go home, they'll venture to the mailbox, then around the block, then two blocks, then to the park. The work students do in your classroom, just like rehabilitation and recovery, takes time and practice.

Rather than thinking about leaps and bounds, focus instead on taking tiny steps every day. In a process-driven environment, many factors beyond grades keep students motivated. Some students have intrinsic motivation, some are motivated by an authentic purpose, and others by a goal they've set for themselves. By shifting the focus away from grades and toward an environment of improvement, students will innately want to do well. By not focusing only on an outcome, students will relax. In this freedom, they will be eager and more able to show their best—to themselves and to those around them.

Teachers and students are not perfect, but we can show up for each other, encourage one another, collaborate, and commit to the process. Learning is a marathon—not a sprint—and it's the culmination of average days that leads to greatness.

WHAT YOU CAN DO TOMORROW

The best teachers are themselves learners, experimenters, and creatives. The following prompts will help you clarify your thoughts and dissect your current classroom to understand what works and what needs to change so you can start to transition to a process-based learning environment.

- **Evaluate your classroom.** What is your subject's process? In what ways is your classroom outcome-based and process-based? Analyze your classroom structures and procedures. What do your systems communicate to students? What is most important? How do your students currently use a process? Do you want your students to get an A or to find a passion for the subject—or both? Set aside quiet time to think about these questions and your answers.

- **Understand how the process works for you.** Identify times when you used a process and how you can implement similar concepts in your classroom. I recently collaborated on decorative quilts. My mom wanted to recycle old fabrics, and I wanted to display art in my home. In creating quilts, my mom cut out colored rectangles. Together, we placed them on the floor in a pleasing arrangement. Then we sought feedback. As my dad and boyfriend critiqued, my mom and I listened, without taking offense, and revised our designs. There was no right or wrong way to construct the quilt; there was only what we thought worked best with the pieces we had. (See Image 1.2.) This technique can be a blue-print for implementing a process-based assessment classroom model: attempt, ask for feedback, revise, try something new, and repeat.

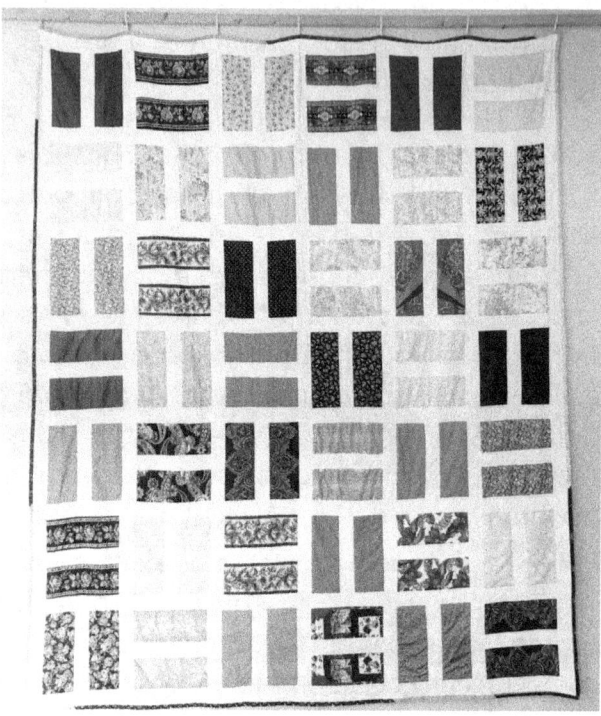

Image 1.2

- **Set a lofty goal.** As a practitioner, what do you value? Values drive your classroom's process-based structure. As you think about your values, notice how they align with your school, district, and community. Consider your values along with your answers to the questions in the first bullet point, and then set a big, lofty goal. It's okay if you change this goal later—you just need a place to start.

After you've set an initial goal, think about what processes will lead students to their best performances. How can you engineer an environment that will make these performances possible? What habits will students practice, learn, or develop? How will you know when you've achieved your goal?

- **Ask students to set a goal.** A student-driven goal sets a purpose. It fosters an environment where students can choose to commit and allows the teacher and the student to collaborate on a shared vision and work in a process-based environment together.

  Guide students to write and place their goals where they can refer to them each day. Maybe it's a heading that shows up on all their Google Docs. Maybe the goal is written on a sticky note, placed on their computer or desk, or added to the top of their class binder. Consider displaying each student's goal on your classroom walls or on a bulletin board. Sharing goals with teachers, classmates, parents, and friends helps hold students accountable.

  Student goal examples:

  ▸ Ask questions when I am confused or need more information.

  ▸ Share with a partner before requesting the teacher's feedback.

  ▸ Contribute to a classroom discussion once a week.

A BLUEPRINT FOR FULL IMPLEMENTATION

To create a process-based environment in your classroom, identify problems, accept limitations, consider controllables, gather support, act on the best solution, evaluate, repeat, and share. This way of assessing is not a one-time fix; it is a cycle that will be re-evaluated and modified.

Step 1: Identify problems.

Start by understanding your circumstances and what you are unable to change. Pinpoint limitations and anticipate roadblocks. Play devil's advocate. Forecast what the naysayers may say. Map out the reality of your school structures, your schedule, and your job responsibilities. Flesh out possible roadblocks to a process-based classroom. Pinpointing obstacles is the first step to engineering creative solutions.

Step 2: Accept limitations.

Are you required to give a grade at the end of the quarter? Do you have to prepare students for state testing? Is your curriculum predetermined? Don't be distracted by the uncontrollables; instead, accept your situation so you can spend energy on what you can control. Even within grade-based structures, you can create a process-based environment and assess the process.

Step 3: Consider controllables.

Outline multiple ways to implement process-based assessments. What is possible? How could you build a process-based classroom? How could you assess students on their abilities to use and move through habits? Without judgment, brainstorm as many solutions as you can. Consider your content and curriculum, your school schedule, your school and district grading policies and requirements, the number of students in your classroom, and parent expectations. Explore what could serve as benchmarks or targets within your content area; how students could move through the process, both independently and collaboratively; and how that process could be assessed.

What instructional strategies could you use to help students practice skills? If you have a specific skill in mind, focus the entire process on that skill, including your assessments. Remember: you don't need to assess everything; you can focus on one part of the process.

Step 4: Gather support.

Experts and allies will be willing to assist, share their experiences, or champion your efforts. Allies can be found at conferences or on social media. You may also be able to learn from other educators through journal articles or blog posts. Start by reaching out to colleagues or sources you admire or want to learn from. Invite department members to engage in conversations and join you in learning more about building student learning habits through a process-based environment.

IF YOUR DISTRICT REQUIRES YOU TO SET GOALS, BUILD PROCESS-BASED ASSESSMENT INTO THOSE GOALS.

Big accomplishments don't happen all at once; they take patience and dedication. Discuss with your administration what you're considering. If your district requires you to set goals, build process-based assessment into those goals. In addition to being detailed and measurable, the goal should express the desired impact on student learning. What are students expected to demonstrate? How can student performances differ to allow each to succeed?

The following are examples of teacher-generated goals:

- By the end of the school year, students will learn and implement strategies to improve their confidence.

- Students will know the benefits of a growth mindset and practice metacognition so they can persevere through challenges.

- By the end of the second quarter, students will be better able to communicate scientific information (e.g., experimental design, data reporting, data analysis, and conclusions).

- Students will assess their ability to be self-directed with the goal of becoming independent learners.

- Using process-based assessment, students will engage with the writing process daily.

- Using a writers' workshop format, students will use feedback and revision to improve their writing.

Review your desired results, specific indicators, or incremental targets and how you will measure the results. Results do not have to be grades; results can be anecdotal or observational. Results can also be student responses to surveys or student work. Consider how you might measure student progress and how best to articulate that progress to an outsider.

Step 5: Act.

You are your classroom's expert. Only you know what works best for your subject area, grade, and schedule and for the individual students and families within your community.

The team of writing teachers at my school started out using rubrics, then we shifted to a four-point system, then to a three-point system. After attending conferences, we aimed to go gradeless. Finally, we settled on a process-point system. Even this is not the perfect solution, but it is what works best right now. Don't think of your action as a solution. It is just the start of your own process.

Step 6: Evaluate and repeat.

After you try a method, continue discussions and experiment with better ways to engage students in the process of learning and growing.

Continually come back to identify problems, accept limitations, consider controllables, gather support, and act on the best solution.

Step 7: Share.

Invite the community of teachers around you to learn about and use process-based assessment. Select artifacts that can work as your evidence. Artifacts may show implementation (what was done) or its impact (how it made a difference). Consider writing samples, student portfolios, lab reports, student self-evaluations, classwork, student projects, or exit slip responses. You may also include your curriculum map, standards, lesson plans, teacher calendar or timeline, activities, games, or assignments. Publish your experiences in blog posts or articles. Post them to your social media pages. Add a vignette to your school's newsletter. Share anecdotes at department meetings. Present at conferences. Share the joy and successes of a process-based classroom.

OVERCOMING PUSHBACK

Grades can be polarizing and triggering. Honor cords, car insurance discounts, scholarships, and college admissions depend on grades, and parents, colleagues, and students are used to systems that value outcomes. When adopting a process-based assessment model, expect pushback from those who do not yet understand the benefits.

Parents may say, "But how is this graded?" When this question comes up, invite students to join the conversation. Ask students to share their goals with their parents or guardians and describe how they work through their processes in class and how their processes are evaluated. The students' voices, sharing their own daily habits, allow parents to understand the focus is on learning and growing, not on perfection or outcomes.

Colleagues may say, "But aren't you just grading on effort?" Explain the difference between effort and helping students build habits of learning. It's difficult to know how much effort a student puts in. But by helping them build daily learning habits, you will witness their learning processes and gather evidence of their learning and growth. Listen to colleagues and welcome their feedback and suggestions. Invite them to share ideas on how each of you can improve your teaching and build a process-based school culture where students are excited to learn.

Students will say, "But what do I need to do to get an A?" Be honest with your students and discuss the benefits of process-based goals rather than grade-based outcomes. Remind them that learning is less about being right or wrong and more about identifying what works and what doesn't. Show students that if they work through the process, they will not only get an A but, more importantly, improve themselves.

THE HACK IN ACTION

Anthony Christian teaches metal fabrication, a welding class, to juniors and seniors. In his class, students gain the skills needed to weld professionally. "But it's not about getting it done right the first time," he says.

Christian starts each weldment (two pieces of metal joined together) with a fifteen-to-twenty-minute lesson. He follows that with a demonstration in which he sometimes makes mistakes on purpose. (See Image 1.3.)

"I want to alert my students to visual cues or highlight sounds that will lead to flaws or discontinuity," he says. "Demoing validates my skill for the students—but messing up helps students realize that they can stand on their own two feet, even if they don't get it done perfectly."

Image 1.3: Teacher Anthony Christian demonstrates
metal fabrication techniques for a student.

As students experiment with welding, Christian sits by their side. He watches as some fail four or five times before they get it right; others, he says, fail a dozen times. Along the way, Christian gives direct, verbal feedback. He shows students how to recognize the beginning foundations that need refinement and to keep working toward mastery. He says students who take the tips and tricks he gives them move toward achievement.

Throughout the semester, Christian slowly removes his scaffolding and asks students to figure things out on their own.

"It's about getting students to be resilient, to figure out why something didn't work, and then to try a different way," he says.

When a student continues to struggle, Christian might demonstrate individually for them again or engage in a discussion.

"I try to encourage a dialogue about the process," he says, "to help them go through their frustrations. It's about helping each student come up with a method to their madness, to help them through self-discovery."

His classroom culture allows students to work through the process as many times as needed to learn the skill. An assessment chart hangs on his classroom door. Each student's name is listed vertically, and the skills are listed horizontally. For each skill, students can earn a ✓-, ✓, or ✓+. Because Christian works within a traditional grading system, his students know a ✓- is 60 percent, a ✓ is 85 percent, and a ✓+ is 100 percent.

He says, "Most students don't even bring me bad stuff. They know the industry standard and what needs to change to achieve that."

Christian wants students to realize there's no right or wrong way to get the outcome, but it's about figuring out what works for each student's process. He learned about this process-based assessment strategy when he took a class at a local technical college. His instructors wanted to produce successful welders; they wanted to train students who could walk onto a job site and succeed. Christian wants the same.

"Each student may get to the end result a different way, but in the end, they learn how to increase their chances at nailing it every time," he says. "It's not about getting it done but about learning the process."

Focusing on the process benefits students, as it allows them to take control of their learning. It shifts the focus away from earning grades and toward building constructive, daily habits. Students understand they will occasionally backslide in some skills as they expand in others. They learn to view those shifts as part of the process.

By assessing student learning processes, we invite diversity in learning styles and needs as students move forward, invest, take risks, learn from failure, challenge rules, stay curious, collaborate, and persevere.

ENCOURAGE PRACTICE, NOT PERFECTION
Spur Performance with Daily Habits

You will never change your life until you change something you do daily. The secret of your success is found in your daily routine.
— JOHN C. MAXWELL, AUTHOR, SPEAKER, AND PASTOR

THE PROBLEM: Students procrastinate and forfeit the benefits of accumulated, daily practice

MANY OF OUR students sit in classrooms, stuck in idle, listening to (or maybe tuning out) their teachers. Then, they leave with homework. Problems to solve, measures to practice, essays to write. But first: a club meeting or sports practice, then work and dinner or care for siblings. By the time they can start on the homework, they're tired. And overwhelmed. They'd much rather stream a sports game or watch a movie or check social media, so they rush through their homework. They don't experiment or play. They don't commit to or enjoy the process, and they don't dive in. They check the box and call the assignment busywork. Or maybe they don't complete the assignment at all, pushing it off until later or never.

Students, like most humans, do what they feel like doing. But often, this approach does not build successful habits or encourage exploration, play, experimentation, or enjoyment. It does not lead to learning and growing.

● ● ●

Like many moms, Kari wanted her son Luke, a sophomore, to assume ownership of his academic responsibilities. She hoped her hands-off approach would empower Luke to manage his schedule and find processes that worked. She didn't want to micromanage or be a helicopter mom, so she didn't ask about homework, and she didn't follow his progress on his school's learning management system.

With only a few days before final exams, Kari checked Luke's progress. When she saw an F in English, she stormed into her son's room. "I'm taking away your game console and your TV!"

"Don't worry," he said. "I'm going to hand in my late work and get my grade up."

Less than two hours later, Luke asked for his games back. "All my late work is done," he said.

Kari couldn't believe it. How could Luke do a semester's worth of work in two hours? She didn't want to prolong the fight, so she returned his items and waited for the late grades to be entered.

What she saw a few days later infuriated her. Luke's grade jumped to a B.

Kari hoped Luke would salvage a D- and realize he couldn't wait until the last minute to do his work. She wanted him to learn a lesson so that next time, he would execute a plan, implement a productive work ethic, and pay attention to details.

When the late grades were entered, Luke didn't even read the teacher's comments on his essays. He didn't care about any of her feedback. The results confirmed what Luke already knew to be true: he could slack off all semester, rush through late assignments, and pass with an above-average grade. He could get through without learning much.

THE HACK: Encourage practice, not perfection

In *Everybody Writes*, Ann Handley wrote, "We're tempted to think that writing is an art, that only an anointed lucky few can do it well. But that's an excuse—a justification that lets the lazy among us off the hook for being the communication equivalent of a couch potato: flabby, unmotivated, inarticulate. But the truth is that the key to being a better writer is, essentially, to be a more productive one. Or more simply, the key to being a better writer is to write."

The same is true for every content area. Producing is the best form of practice. You want to be better at mathematics? Solve more problems. You want to be a better programmer? Write more programs. You want to run a faster mile? Run more miles.

In high school, Kelly Britt auditioned for every musical theater production, but she never played the lead. Britt said, "I was not a standout kid. I was quiet, and I didn't like to be the center of attention."

While some of her peers quit when they didn't get a starring role, Britt stayed to sing in the chorus. She took private voice lessons, danced in the background, and sometimes painted sets or cleaned dressing rooms. She understood only one person could play the lead role, but everyone could improve by participating in the process of theater.

Britt said her teachers' feedback helped her realize her potential. She said, "During my senior year, my choir directors pulled me aside and said, 'Wow! Your voice has really grown operatically.' That comment was one of a handful that inspired me to start seriously pursuing classical music."

Britt followed her curiosity, and as she studied, she realized how much she didn't know. She said, "Voice lessons led to acting classes, which led to dance classes, hair and makeup tutorials, and language and dialect study, which led to stage combat, which led to a Shakespeare class, and somehow a bit of aerial and acrobatic training got thrown in there at some point as well."

It's been ten years since high school, and now Britt makes her living as an opera singer and actress. She realized her best outcome—to be a professional performer—by training herself daily in skills and habits. She says, "I wasn't the best at any of it by a long shot, but that's the beauty of the arts—you just have to bring yourself to the table and trust all the work you've done to get there."

● ● ●

Remind students that no one will be good at an activity the first time they attempt it. Tell them that failure is expected. Failure is where they will start. Students must work through a process to better understand successful habits. Encourage students to stop chasing perfection. There is no perfect, and if they're looking for that, they're only setting themselves up for fear, frustration, or failure.

Aim to help students become "doers." James Clear writes about the compounding effect of production in *Atomic Habits*. He suggests aiming to improve one percent each day. He says, "If you get one percent better each day for one year, you'll end up thirty-seven times better by the time you're done." Small, consistent efforts build exponential gains.

Instead of grading students on effort (which we cannot possibly begin to measure) or perfection (which is not possible), assess them on their ability to work through the process of practicing, sharing, contributing, and improving.

Take a cue from the track team. When an athlete joins the team, they may want to be a four-hundred-meter runner, but the coach asks each athlete to try all the events. All athletes run the mile, the two mile, and the three-hundred-meter hurdles; they high jump and long jump; and they throw the shot and disk. They can learn from each event. As athletes try out events, they discover their strengths and what they enjoy. The coach encourages each athlete to pursue and develop what they do best or most easily. The coach knows bringing out each athlete's best is good for the team and for the individual.

To encourage practice, Speech and Language Pathologist Julie Schroeder finds tasks her elementary school students are already doing.

If students read every day for fifteen minutes, she asks them to read out loud for five of those minutes. If students enjoy making friends laugh, she provides jokes with sounds students need to practice.

Schroeder aims to make practice easy. "At school, I use five-minute articulation sessions," she says. "I used to wonder how I could get anything done in five minutes, but what I've found is that kids make more progress with little bursts of practice. When we're only working for five minutes, there's no time to get frustrated."

Schroeder provides passages for students to read. She records her students and then plays back the recording. As students listen, she presents a picture of a bullseye. Instead of posing a yes-or-no question, Schroeder asks how close the students think they are to the target. Students point to the bullseye to evaluate their own production.

HELP STUDENTS TO PRACTICE AND WORK TOWARD THEIR GOALS WITHOUT FEAR OF FAILURE OR THE PRESSURE OF PERFECTION.

"This makes their self-assessment visual and allows students to critique themselves. They become their own clinician," Schroeder says. "Assessment is never about grading. It is about practice."

Schroeder explains to both students and families that working with sounds is similar to climbing a staircase. The first step on the staircase is about getting the sound. Once they've climbed that step, Schroeder can help students practice at the word level, the phrase level, and the sentence level. At the top of the staircase are reading and speaking in conversation and being spontaneous with word sounds. During Schroeder's sessions with students, she focuses on taking one step on the staircase and making a bit of progress at a time.

In addition to the students' self-assessments, Schroeder incorporates her feedback plus comments from family members and teachers. Gathering data from several sources helps Schroeder modify her lessons to better assist each student's practice.

Similarly, athletes often gather input and data from others and adjust their training in order to improve. In the London 2012 Olympic triathlon, athlete Gwen Jorgensen suffered a flat tire on her bike. This setback pushed her to evaluate her process and find out what she could do better. What did the consistent podium finishers do that she didn't? How could she improve her chance of winning gold at the Rio 2016 Olympics?

In her research, Jorgensen found a common denominator: the most successful people (whether athletes, authors, actors, or academics) surround themselves daily with others who are chasing similar goals. They work side by side with coaches and teammates, they collaborate, they learn from others, and they try and fail. Then the next day, they apply what they learned and try again. She found that ultra-achievers placed themselves in situations that challenged them each day.

Jorgensen knew she needed a daily performance environment if she wanted to win the gold medal. She researched groups and discovered an international squad of triathletes who lived, worked, and recovered together in Australia. She joined them and, less than four years later, crossed the finish line as the Rio 2016 Olympic Triathlon Champion.

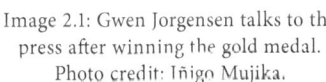

Image 2.1: Gwen Jorgensen talks to the press after winning the gold medal. Photo credit: Iñigo Mujika.

Image 2.2: Gwen Jorgensen and her coach, Jamie Turner. Photo credit: Iñigo Mujika.

Athletes and students who find success will be the ones who set a goal and put in the work. They will practice and execute habits day after day. It's like the stonecutter's credo (credited to Jacob Riis) that states, "When nothing seems to help, I go and look at a stonecutter hammering away at his rock perhaps a hundred times without as much as a crack showing in it. Yet at the hundred and first blow, it will split in two, and I know it was not that blow that did it, but all that had gone before."

Jorgensen uses this credo as a metaphor to help her perform. She says, "I'm not looking at the day-to-day improvement but the week-to-week and then month-to-month. That's the key to me being 100 percent."

She says, "High performance is often seen as training, facilities, staff, culture, and equipment all combined to create winning, [but] perhaps it's best defined as a behavior."

What behaviors do your students need to practice in your classroom?

WHAT YOU CAN DO TOMORROW

To immerse students in a daily performance environment, inspire them to set process-driven goals. Help students to practice and work toward their goals without fear of failure or the pressure of perfection. Have conversations that encourage students to commit to a process over an outcome.

- **Engage students in a dialogue.** Ask them questions to prompt reflection about their daily learning habits. Consider the following questions:
  - ‣ What are your strengths and weaknesses?
  - ‣ What do you want to work on in this class?
  - ‣ What processes can help you make progress on your goals?
  - ‣ How will you assess the effectiveness of a process?
  - ‣ What limitations do you need to consider?
  - ‣ What are the roles of the teacher and your classmates in committing to your process?
  - ‣ How will you know when your process is successful?
  - ‣ What will trigger a re-evaluation or modification to your process?

- **Help them identify their process goals.** Ask students to set process-driven goals for themselves. These are the habits they learn to cultivate and to pay attention to. Ask students to consider the following:

  ‣ What behaviors will you repeat each day?

  ‣ Where do you need to focus your time?

  Here are examples of student process goals in three areas:

  Choir

  ‣ Sing with proper posture.

  ‣ Relax jaw on vowel sounds.

  ‣ Listen to peers and work to create a pleasing blend.

  Physical education

  ‣ Pack gym clothes before going to bed.

  ‣ Increase water intake.

  ‣ Get eight hours of uninterrupted sleep.

  Elementary school

  ‣ Review spelling word flashcards each night for ten minutes.

  ‣ Organize papers by class.

  ‣ Ask questions when confused.

- **Encourage students to practice.** If students struggle to produce or use class time effectively, try these four tactics:

> ▸ Ask them to rewrite the problem or task.
> Phrasing the problem in their own way may
> reveal possible solutions.

> ▸ Return to their process goals; remind students
> of their vision and their motivation.

> ▸ Ask them to map out the processes that will
> help them reach their vision and to generate
> possible solutions to combat gridlock.

> ▸ Place students in groups. Seeing others be
> productive can exert powerful pressure.

A BLUEPRINT FOR FULL IMPLEMENTATION

Athletes join teams and work with personal trainers. Singers get vocal coaches and audition for ensembles. Writers use editors and bring their work to writers' workshops. Teachers attend professional development workshops and connect with colleagues through social media threads. Help your students connect with others and build habits that encourage practice, not perfection.

Step 1: Instill a predictable routine.

Consider the rule of thirds when framing your classroom's daily structure: one-third instruction, one-third application or practice, and one-third collaboration.

Students crave structure and thrive with clear expectations. A structure provides the mechanism that enables each student's process to work. To improve, students need dedicated time to learn, practice, and collaborate. As they work, walk around the room and ask questions.

Instill classroom processes that lead to evaluation and progression. Predictable processes keep your system moving. In a writing class, students expect to study a concept, see an example that uses that concept, try the concept, and then share what they tried with the class or a partner. Since each student has a different writing process, encourage them to trust their gut, take a risk, relax, and figure it out by trying and doing. Give them time to share their practice and receive feedback.

- What can students expect the process to look like in your classroom?
- What stimuli will trigger desirable behaviors?
- What habits will build successful processes in your content area?

Step 2: Give students a time limit.

Require students to be productive during your time together; this holds them accountable to their process. Collect work at the end of class. You do not need to grade the work you collect. Instead, assess it. Ask students to note on the assignment where and what kind of feedback they'd like, where they are struggling, what process they used successfully, or how the task relates to their goal. These notes will help you provide meaningful feedback (more about feedback in Hack 6: Generate Feedback Loops); they also allow the students to own their processes.

Step 3: View practice as progress.

There's no such thing as perfect practice. And practice doesn't make perfect. Instead, remind students they are working for today's best. Be honest with students about how each day's best differs depending on the circumstances or the task at hand. We all have days when our plans just don't work out. Some assignments won't resonate with certain students, or some days, a student will be distracted by a personal issue. This is okay. Conversations build trust with students and allow them to realize you are not there to downgrade and judge but to collaborate with and help them progress, learn, and grow.

Step 4: Ask students to revisit their goals.

Revising goals helps students evaluate their process and allows teachers and students to work collaboratively toward reaching them. Remind students that their processes are ever-changing. Students, like their teachers, need to be adaptable and open to modifications. Guide students to ask themselves these questions at least monthly:

- What progress have I made?
- What do I still need to do?
- What processes will lead to better progress or performances?

Step 5: Assess the practice.

Instead of evaluating an outcome (like homework problems or a paper, test, or quiz), assess experiences, experimentation, and daily habits.

Experiences
When students hear a guest speaker, you could assess them on their ability to submit thoughtful, content-related questions or to write a thank-you note with specific take-aways from the presentation.

> *IMPLEMENT A GRADING STRUCTURE THAT VALUES IMPROVEMENT OVER OUTCOMES. REWARD STUDENTS FOR TRYING, WHICH IS HOW THEY LEARN.*

Experimentation
You could assess students by examining, observing, or testing ways to approach a problem or project.

Daily habits
When students analyze models, they could observe techniques or state what they noticed about how a problem was solved. Students could be assessed on their ability to implement a habit (daily vocabulary words from your content area, a weekly puzzle or game, or a daily motivational reading). Consider assessing students' answers to

this question at the end of the lesson: How were you passionate and productive today?

Don't let perfect be the enemy of good. Instead, implement a grading structure that values improvement over outcomes. Reward students for trying, which is how they learn. Encourage students to build a daily imperfect practice. Consider accommodating challenging days by dropping the lowest score each quarter or allowing students to decide when they are ready for assessment. You might also enter scores when students prompt you to. Consider adding scores to your gradebook with a zero weight. Averaging scores is counterintuitive to a growth or practice mindset.

OVERCOMING PUSHBACK

Students learn by doing. Daily, provide time in class for students to go through the process of learning, applying, and sharing. Implement a daily performance structure that will focus your students on moving forward, collaborating, and growing rather than on earning grades. But expect pushback from master procrastinators and excuse-makers.

Students don't use in-class work time. Help students build in-class habits they can rely on. Once the process is a habit, their passion and excitement will kick in. This will elevate their use of in-class time and make the process automatic. The learning habit becomes ingrained, expected, and second nature.

Compliment and praise students for their efforts. Send notes and emails home to students and their guardians when you see positive behaviors. Sugar is more effective than spice. See Image 2.3 for an example of a postcard note I wrote to a student.

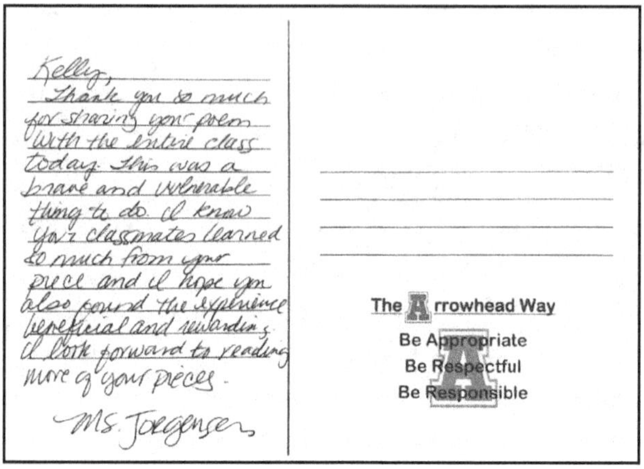

Kelly,
Thank you so much for sharing your poem with the entire class today. This was a brave and vulnerable thing to do. I know your classmates learned so much from your piece and I hope you also found the experience beneficial and rewarding. I look forward to reading more of your pieces.
Ms. Jorgensen

The Arrowhead Way
Be Appropriate
Be Respectful
Be Responsible

Image 2.3

Here are a handful of parent responses to my notes home:

> "Thank you for the kind message. She showed us her poem Tuesday night, and we really enjoyed hearing it from her. She really enjoys your class."

> "Thank you SO very much for reaching out to us! What a wonderful, wonderful email to receive. She is a great kid. She has had some emotional struggles over the past few years, and it has been a big hurdle for her. I've noticed this year in particular she has really been making an effort with her school work. I very much appreciate hearing you validate how much her hard work is paying off. I will be sure to share this with her and tell her how very proud we are of her!"

> "Thanks for the good news, Liz. It's nice to hear about something positive; I appreciate it. I will ask them to share their work with me and will encourage them. Thanks again."

> "She has been sharing her writing with us, and I have been so impressed with her work! I am so glad to hear from you about this! Of course, I think it's good, but to hear it from you is awesome. She shared with me your comments this

a.m. about her recent poem. She was so excited! I have never seen her so pumped about a subject in school before, so keep up the awesome work motivating her and we will do the same. Thanks again!"

Each parent's reply gave me a boost and reminded me of the positive impact I'm having. The students, too, appreciated my efforts:

"Thanks for emailing my dad."

"My mom was so excited to see your email."

"My mom took me to Culver's for custard because of what you wrote."

I aim to email a different group of parents for each assignment.

That sounds nice, but some students still don't use in-class work time. Some students are not used to putting in work each day or being held accountable to a daily performance environment. Instead, they're used to procrastinating and making excuses. You may have students who resist or flat-out refuse to work in class. They might be worried about failing. They might be afraid of the grade they'll receive if they work in class. In these instances, consider sharing a pizza analogy with your students. When it's pizza night at home, I don't mull over toppings. Instead, I open the fridge and pantry and see what's available. Green olives, sausage, and red peppers? Spinach, goat cheese, and onions? It doesn't really matter; it's about deciding and then getting the pizza on the table. Only once the pizza is made can I decide if I like it. Only then will I receive my family's feedback and be able to improve next time. Likewise, all you're asking students to do is use the provided work time to focus on their process. Encourage them to experiment.

Seriously, some students *still* don't use in-class work time. Remind students that a slow start is better than no start. Encourage them to think about class time like they would an athletic practice. For coaches, students go to practice and participate. They perform, and although some days are better than others, they show up and give their best effort. Perhaps students can consider how basketball players practice their skills daily. If they miss all their free throws, that's okay. The coach might be disappointed, but she would come over and talk. She would encourage the player, provide tips, and remind them about positive habits. If the athlete had decided not to shoot free throws— or not to participate in practice—because they might miss the basket, then they wouldn't have a chance to hear encouragement, apply their learnings, and ultimately succeed. Help students realize that the process of practice is what makes a more successful, well-rounded player—and student. It's what allows for improvement.

Athletes can't go back and shoot yesterday's free throws or get into yesterday's scrimmage. They can't practice yesterday's skills. Those experiences are gone, and there is no way to recreate them. It's the same with class time. Students have to show up each day, practice, and participate. Only then can they benefit from feedback and improve. Only then can they gain from the cumulative nature of practice.

If students still refuse to work, contact someone at home. Get students and parents on the same page to strengthen the team. If possible, call rather than email. Emails can easily lead to misunderstandings. Even better: schedule a video or face-to-face meeting. This allows parents to see facial expressions and hear genuine care and concern. Put the student in control of the conference. Start by asking the student to 1) explain the class, 2) state why they're struggling, and 3) explain their plan to turn things around. Parents are often able to offer solutions, as they know their child best. At the end of the conversation, schedule a follow-up discussion to review progress.

See Appendix D for an example of an email I wrote to a parent and CC'd his two students, and Appendix E for an example of a positive note I sent to a parent whose student volunteered to read a poem out loud.

THE HACK IN ACTION

Rick Witte teaches The Leader's Mindset to high school students in grades nine through twelve. Witte says, "When I was a younger teacher, I believed I could use outcomes to make students excited about learning. We do this a lot in schools. We believe we can move students with external motives. I have come to see this as a myth. My class is structured to make the following truth of life clear: no one can make anyone else do anything. I try to facilitate an understanding that students are making choices all day that matter to them and everyone around them. Although it seems as if choices lead to outcomes, this is simply not the case. Our choices become our processes by which we lead our lives. In The Leader's Mindset, I emphasize what we can control—the process—and move away from uncontrollables like outcomes."

At the beginning of every year, Witte gathers data from his students. One question he asks is: "What goals do you have for the school year?"

Most responses focus on outcomes: "Straight A's," "A GPA of 3.5 or above," "All A's and B's," "Get good enough grades to get into (insert dream university)," and "Score well on the ACT."

Witte finds this troubling because students do not control outcomes. They can influence them with their habits, but ultimately, students do not get to decide which grade they earn, which ACT score they receive, or which university they get into.

To help students understand just how important it is to put process over outcomes, he removes grades. When he created this class, Witte spoke with his school administration and discovered assessment alternatives to A, B, C, D, and F. He researched what assessment looked like in other departments, spoke to teachers, and decided pass/fail would remove the emphasis on "getting an A."

As a pass/fail elective, the course The Leader's Mindset allows students to dive into the material and the process, not manipulate the environment to achieve a prize outside of their control.

He said, "When I first mention The Leader's Mindset class is pass/fail, there is a palpable feeling in the room of confusion and maybe even a little anger. We circle back to why the class is not graded as we move through the semester, and these conversations revolve around the idea of controlling the controllables—and outcomes are not controllable."

In The Leader's Mindset, the process focuses on a daily routine. When students come to class, they remove their phone, get note packets out, write down recovery scores, press pause, practice gratitude, and receive the daily dare. Because each step is important to the process, Witte makes time for them every day.

Witte says students are used to only celebrating outcomes—and good ones, at that. He says, "Students will continue to chase whatever is celebrated. We are all wired this way." To break students from this, Witte often says during class, "We need your mistakes today." In The Leader's Mindset, he emphasizes practice over perfection.

Witte says, "When all we do is celebrate when things go well, students will try to avoid mistakes and failure. In The Leader's Mindset, the students and I celebrate everything involved in our process. Sure, things go exactly as planned sometimes, and we celebrate those days. However, mistakes and failure are very much a part of the learning process too. In fact, they are vital, and learning does not happen without them. I tell students that if they leave my class without ever having felt uncomfortable, I wasted their time."

Schools, by default, are outcome-based organizations. Witte says students come into his class with an idea of what they think they need in order to find success. It takes an immense amount of work in relationship-building to get them to break from that script. Witte says if he's asking his students to get uncomfortable and embrace failure, then they have to know he cares.

"I try to help students understand that their choices matter, their routines matter, and that they both are owned by them. Ultimately students should come to school and uniquely create. Schools should exist to facilitate this journey for students to help them begin finding their own processes in life," he says.

Daily production leads to increased confidence. It also gives students examples of their work to share and improve. Instill predictable routines that allow practice to accumulate.

Emphasize daily habits that lead to improved performances. In a writing class, guide students to write for ten minutes at the beginning of class. They learn new concepts, implement them in pieces, and then have time to share. In a choir class, ask students to spend ten minutes warming up before rehearsal. They follow a posted schedule for the bulk of their rehearsal and then have two minutes for questions and reminders.

Candice Elliott, a personal finance writer, states, "Research shows that the overwhelming majority of experts who reach the top of their fields (for instance, chess grandmasters or great composers) have spent *a minimum* of ten years acquiring and honing their skills." Of course, our students cannot accumulate these years of practice in the time they share with us, but they can begin putting in the work. They can focus on improving by investing in daily practice. They can be "doers." They can work at being one percent better each day.

Daily, provide students with specific tasks and allow them space to practice their habits. A daily environment removes the I'll-do-it-later mentality and reinforces the compounding power of imperfect practice.

RELINQUISH CONTROL
Adopt a How-Driven Classroom

That's the whole secret: to do things that excite you.
— RAY BRADBURY, AUTHOR

THE PROBLEM: Teachers feel stuck in an outdated, outcome-based teaching model

THE FOLLOWING SCENARIO is all too familiar: You prepare students for a state-mandated test. You know it's a waste of time, but you still try your best to prepare them. You've set an external scorecard to measure yourself; you want each student in the top fiftieth percentile. To achieve your goal, you bombard them with material. You forgo hands-on experiences or labs. You rush through concepts, but you touch on every topic you anticipate will be tested. You know this isn't the best practice, and your goal feels arbitrary and artificial, but you're not sure what else to do; you want your students to score well and to make themselves and their grown-ups proud.

When test day comes, uncontrollables sabotage your efforts. One student was up all night worrying about his parents' divorce; another forgot breakfast; one fought with a friend on social media; another missed the bus.

After the test, students tell you they were asked about concepts they'd never heard of.

When you don't achieve your desired outcomes, a negative mindset nestles in. *Why did I even try? I was always going to fail my students. I am not good enough. I am not smart enough. I am not worthy of being a teacher.*

In this scenario, two factors occurred: circumstances outside your control affected student performance, and students lacked process skills that could have improved their scores. Here are a few of the problems with outcome-focused thinking:

FOCUS ON LEARNING AND PRACTICING RATHER THAN ON OUTCOMES OR GRADES.

- places the teacher in control

- disengages students from learning and retaining

- stalls processes

- circumvents plans that could lead to improvement

- subjects everyone involved to uncontrollables

THE HACK: Relinquish control

Relinquishing control is not about getting students to have the discipline or willpower to complete assignments. It is about helping them construct and practice behaviors that breed improved performances. Students need teachers to help them learn these habits and especially to learn that they are in control of whether they use them.

Focus on learning and practicing rather than on outcomes or grades. Allow your students to analyze. As their teacher, help them to assess:

- *how* things occur instead of *what* occurs

- their daily processes instead of their final products

- the habits that engineer progress

A process-based classroom instills daily habits, increases student confidence, and enables students to make deliberate decisions. We never know what will happen, but we can help students create confidence when they know they're prepared. Daily habits give students the systems for success. These systems are the same for achievement in school and also in the workforce and in life.

Students cannot control outcomes. However, they can control their processes. They can build and implement constructive habits. As teachers, we can ask questions, collaborate with our students, and focus on learning and growing together. Ask students to help you brainstorm a list of behaviors they *can* control. See an example in Image 3.1.

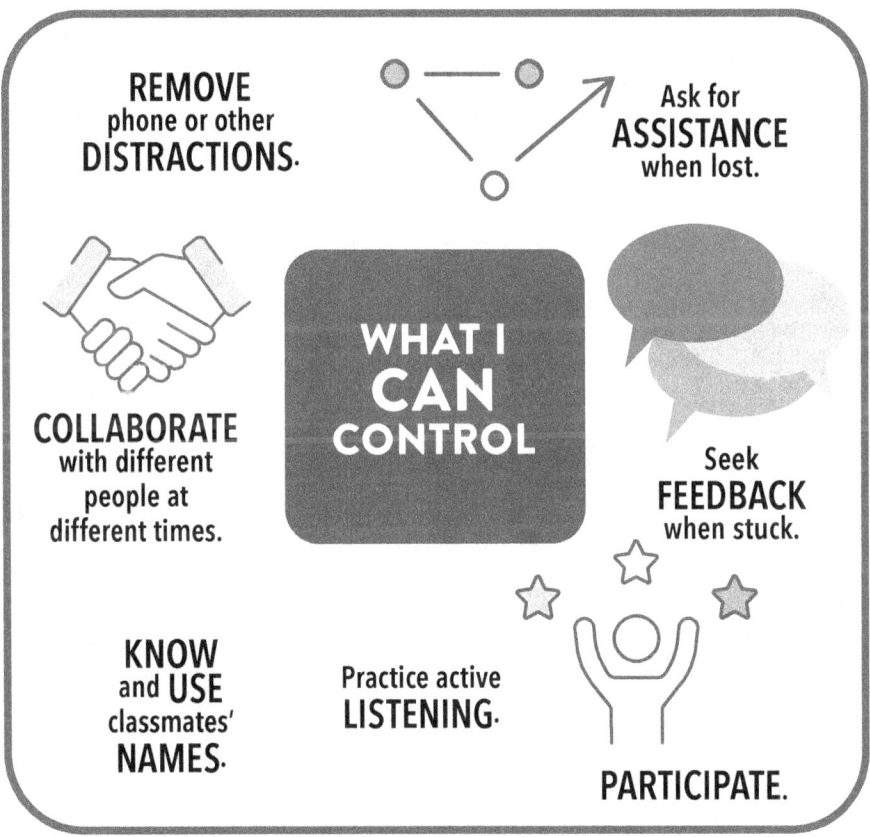

Image 3.1

Our goal should be to encourage students to own their learning: their tangled, mistake-heavy processes. Students need time and space to practice. They also must believe they are capable of success. Instead of getting bogged down with grading, requirements, and restrictions, help students identify *how* to complete a task. By not focusing on the outcome, students will surprise you with their originality, creativity, and risk-taking. What they produce will be beyond any outcome you could have set for them. Students get to control the many ways to approach a problem. As their teacher, refrain from micromanaging as students practice. Instead, allow them to explore and find their own path.

When you relinquish control, you allow students to learn from habits and to construct better performances. Consider when music students audition for the State Honors Choir. Students can audition as early as their freshman year, but most freshmen don't. They don't have the vocal maturity, sight-reading skills, or poise to handle this high-level audition. However, many choir directors encourage talented individuals to do it anyway, as much is learned in the process. Students practice sight-reading skills, prepare a Class A Solo, study with a professional accompanist, and work on aural drills. Students have choices (which song they prepare, who plays the accompaniment) and control their preparation (how often they practice, who they work with).

By the time they arrive at the audition, freshmen have improved through their practice and technique-building. It is not about successfully making the Honors Choir but about the audition itself being a learning experience. Even if a freshman doesn't make the cut, they learned how to handle themselves in a professional setting; they experienced the pressure of singing for a judge; and they sight-read, singing a strange combination of notes, under pressure, with no practice.

Freshmen often appear nervous, forget words, or are surprised by the sight-reading. They don't perform their best under pressure, but they come away with knowledge, experience, and a list of skills they want to improve.

When choir directors sign up freshmen for the experience, they know many freshmen will fail, but directors understand how much the students learn by trying. You can't simulate a real live audition—an authentic experience is the only way to practice. So choir directors support student efforts, guide their preparation, help them analyze the experience, and encourage them to try again. Not surprisingly, many of the students who failed the audition as freshmen go on to join the Honors Choir as sophomores or juniors.

● ● ●

Trina Dodge said her junior and senior advanced algebra class was notorious for exhibiting challenging behaviors. Students acted out, refused to try, or invented excuses. She said, "Students in advanced algebra say they hate math. I often hear them say, 'I can't do it.' They aren't in the advanced math track, so by the time they reach my classroom, they feel behind. The expectations and pressure at my school are so high that students don't realize they're really good math students."

Dodge wants each student to know they aren't behind but just on a different path. To better guide, support, and embrace imperfections, she flipped her classroom. What students once completed in class, they started doing at home. And what students previously did as homework, they started working through with her in class.

At home, students watched ten-to-fifteen-minute recordings of Dodge. They took notes on concepts she explained or jotted down questions to ask the next day. Students told her they appreciated being able to pause her lectures or rewatch sections.

Dodge said flipping her classroom puts students in charge of their own progress. "Students decide if they'll watch the recording. If they don't, they know they'll be a bit behind the next day," she said. "But that's okay. That's their choice." This practice lends itself to relinquishing control and putting the impetus for learning onto the student.

In the classroom the following day, Dodge starts by fielding questions. Then, she leads her students through a "your turn"—a math problem they work through together using the previous night's lecture. "I am helping my students realize that I don't expect them to be math masters, but I want them to know they can do the work," she said.

"It takes out the behavior issues. Now I have very limited classroom management concerns because the excuses have been eliminated," she said. "Going through the problems together, after kids have watched a lecture, doesn't allow them to get stuck. They know together we will accomplish the problems. They're not chasing an impossible task alone."

HELP STUDENTS TO FOCUS ON WHAT'S CONTROLLABLE— TO OWN THEIR PROCESSES AND DO LITTLE THINGS RIGHT, DAY AFTER DAY.

Once students answer questions and tackle problems, they use the remaining class time to start new problems, complete assessments, or work through practice problems. She said her flipped classroom structure allows every student to start at the same place. "We practice and we get stuck together, but then we overcome that obstacle together," she said.

WHAT YOU CAN DO TOMORROW

A successful classroom fosters controllable, student-driven behaviors. These habits make up each student's process. Help students to focus on what's controllable— to own their processes and do little things right, day after day.

- **Help students identify what they can control.**
  Start by asking students what they may be addicted to: grades, test scores, wins, losses, and others' perceptions. Help them understand these concepts are not controllables. Then, ask students to draw a box and draw a smaller box within it. In the outer box, ask students to list what they cannot change. In the smaller box, ask students to list what they can

change. This helps them start to get in the mindset of identifying what they can change and what they cannot. See Image 3.2 for a sports example from Coach Rick Witte, showing what his basketball players can control (the items inside the box) and cannot control (the items outside the box).

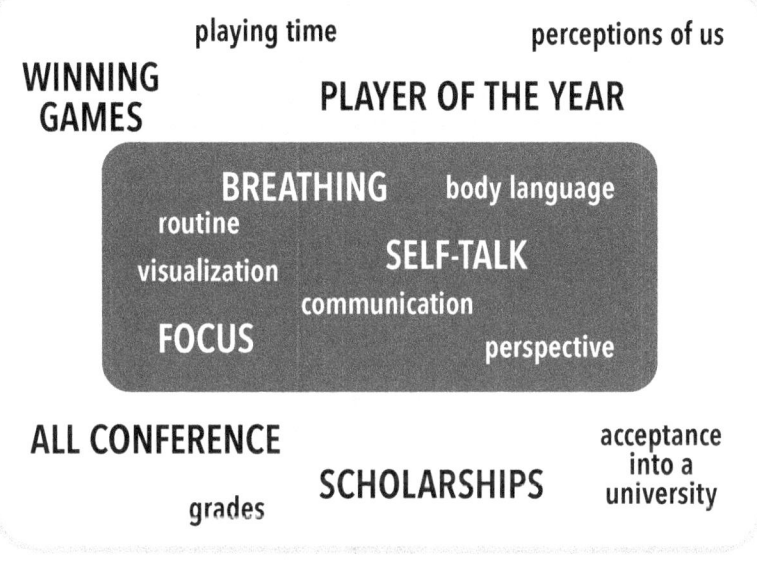

Image 3.2

- **Discuss processes that align with students' values and encourage best performances.** Ask students to identify three processes they can modulate each day. In a physical education class, this may include packing the swimsuit the night before, bringing a full water bottle to class, and using the restroom before leaving the locker room. What processes can help students control the controllables?

This part of the practice is more about identification than execution. How can students de-emphasize the uncontrollables and shift their energy to the controllables? See Image 3.3 for a visual representation of what students can control.

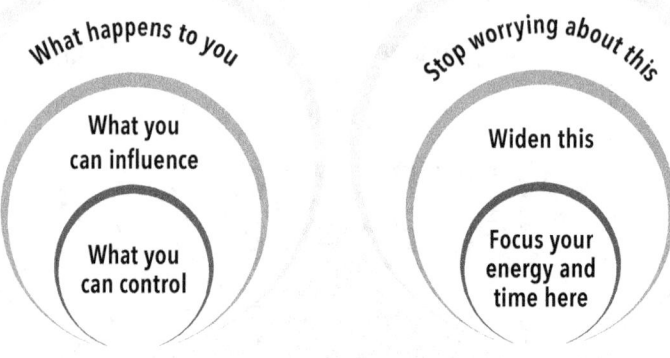

Image 3.3

- **Improve efficiency through practice.** Let students choose what they need to practice and then step aside as they work through the repetitions. The more students practice, the faster they will achieve their desired outcomes. If students expend less energy and get the same outcomes, or if they figure out solutions faster than before, this is progress. The goals are for the action to become second nature and for progress to trend upward. There is always tomorrow to try again. Every day will not be a great day, and progress is not linear. If a day is not productive, remind students that improved efficiency is a form of progress. Students can control their responses and actions; they are powerful over their processes.

- **Assess an exit slip.** Before leaving the classroom, ask students to identify what they controlled or how they applied what they learned. You can also use exit slips for them to recognize the effort of a class-mate or celebrate a good idea.

- **Create process-based charts.** Charts can be specific to your class or include processes outside of class. You can track each student's daily process, but it's better if the student charts their own. Habits are tangible and measurable. Consider a habit chart where you ask students, at the end of each class period, to record what they can control.

  At the top of the process chart, students list their habits. Examples: read for twenty minutes a day, get eight or more hours of sleep, review chemistry notes for fifteen minutes at breakfast, use each spelling word in an original sentence, record homework assignments, drink a hundred ounces of water, pack a bag lunch, and keep a gratitude journal. Encourage students to make their charts visually exciting, giving each item its own color. Once students start tracking habits, they may find a new, positive addiction to checking things off, and they won't want to break the streak. Search online for "habit tracker journal" for ideas to help students design personalized charts.

A BLUEPRINT FOR FULL IMPLEMENTATION

In Hack 1, you identified problems, accepted limitations, considered outcomes, gathered support, and acted on a possible process-based assessment solution. Now it's time to evaluate the solution you implemented. Is it working for students? How can you help students improve their systems?

Step 1: Communicate clearly.

Explain how you assess processes and what you expect from students each day. Place this information not only on the syllabus and your website but also at the top of assignment sheets or in places where students and parents can reference it. Consider how to communicate the expectations and outcomes:

- If you use checkmarks, explain how checkmarks translate to a grade.

- If you use a pass/fail system, explain what determines a pass or fail.

- If you use traditional A-to-F grades, explain how students know when they meet or exceed daily expectations.

Step 2: Redirect students.

As students work, keep them focused on the process by asking these three questions:

- How do you feel about it?

- How do your feelings impact you?

- What helps?

These questions allow students to see that their feelings can be addressed, that they can make a change, and that they can engineer a solution by focusing on the controllables through a planned process.

Consider this scenario that unfolded one day in my creative writing class:

Ms. Jorgensen: "Hi, Jack, I noticed you didn't make progress on your poem last class. Can you tell me a bit about what was going on?"

Jack: "Yeah, I had a chemistry test, and I was studying for it instead of working on my poem."

Ms. Jorgensen: "Did your chemistry test go okay?"

Jack: "No. And now I'm behind in both chemistry and creative writing."

Ms. Jorgensen: "I'm sorry to hear that. How are you feeling right now?"

Jack: "I'm kind of frustrated and mad at myself. Also overwhelmed."

Ms. Jorgensen: "How is this impacting you?"

Jack: "I'm thinking about it a lot."

Ms. Jorgensen: "I imagine I would be doing the same if I were in your shoes. What can you do right now that will help?"

Jack: "I know if I get my poem draft done today in class, I will feel better."

Ms. Jorgensen: "That sounds like a great plan. Do you know what you want to write about?"

Jack: "Yes, I'm writing about a fishing trip."

Ms. Jorgensen: "Awesome! I have only been fishing a few times, so I'm sure I will learn more about fishing from your poem. How will you start?"

Jack: "I have my document open, and I will use anaphora that I just learned about."

Ms. Jorgensen: "Great! I'll come back in ten minutes to see what strategies you're using and what phrases you came up with."

Step 3: Be patient.

Behavior changes take time. Remove the pressure of expectations and provide assessments that value experiences. The most successful process-based assessment models are balanced and put each student in control of their progress. Account for nonlinear progression in your assessments and consider:

- dropping low scores each week, month, or quarter

- recording scores with zero weight

- using checkmarks or pass/fail

- requiring students to self-assess

- putting students in control of when and how they're assessed

Step 4: Recover.

Rest is as important as production. Growing makes us sore, and we all need time to recover. What can recovery look like for your students? Each day cannot build and build; each day cannot be more. It's as important for students to focus on doing the small things right as it is to recognize when it's time for a break. How can you celebrate progress? How can you build in time each day for laughter and smiles?

When you see students struggle or hear frustration, honor that and change the pace of class. Try these examples:

- Play a quick game.

- Share a story, joke, or inspirational quote.

- Complete a collaborative task (write three sentences and pass it to another student, repeat, and share).

- Draw or spark creativity with hands-on experiences.

- Give students time to share what they've done by describing it to a partner or the entire class.

- Allow time for assistance and affirmation.

Students require time each day to perform but also time to be children. A balanced classroom will build enjoyment and encourage students to return to the work. This improves their processes and their performances. Relinquishing your control cultivates space for awe and wonder, enthusiasm and creativity, breathing and gratitude, and play and joy.

OVERCOMING PUSHBACK

Learning is messy, and our students don't need to sit in rows, be quiet and obedient, and wait for us to reveal what's next. Handing students the power to adopt their own how-driven learning and focus on progressing and improving can feel daunting. But you can do it while addressing standards and curriculum requirements.

But I have to address the standards, and I won't be able to get to everything in my curriculum with so much focus on the process. Look at standards through a process-based lens. Each standard is so vague that you are probably bettering it. Consider the Common Core standards for writing:

- CCSS.ELA-LITERACY.W.11-12.3.C // "Use a variety of techniques …"

- CCSS.ELA-LITERACY.W.11-12.5 // "Develop and strengthen writing as needed by planning, revising, editing, rewriting, or trying a new approach …"

- CCSS.ELA-LITERACY.W.11-12.10 // "Write routinely over extended time frames …"

By empowering students to work through a daily process, you are meeting and exceeding the standards tenfold.

Working the process is like saving money; the more you invest at the beginning, the bigger the return will be in the weeks, months, and years to follow. And the more you focus on the process, the greater freedom your students will have to explore the curriculum and subjects that interest them. This will lead to better practices and performances.

Analyze the number of assignments or experiences you require. There is no right or wrong answer to the number but only data to consider. In orchestra, maybe fewer concerts would give students time to improve their techniques. Perhaps more concerts would provide motivation to improve. Do you want to program a concert in the fall to motivate students to put in the preparation? It's the same with art or writing. Do you want students in your writing class to submit to contests early in the semester to prod them to develop a process? Or do you want to wait until the end of the semester when students' skills and confidence have improved? Try out the options and see what produces the most successful processes.

It will take too much time to change my assessment methods. View your classroom on a micro-scale: one class period at a time. Each day, urge students to practice habits they find enjoyable and fruitful. How you assess their process (or each habit) is less important than the habit you assess.

Changing grading practices isn't as difficult as you think. Be clear and transparent about what you grade, and take it one period at a time. Focus on what is important by assessing only the habits students practiced within your time together. Also know that if it's not working, you can re-evaluate and make changes tomorrow.

When the process isn't successful the first time, kids give up. Failure is only a negative if you or your students make it one. A failure or setback should never end a student's progress; instead, it should start a smarter approach. When a student experiences a road-block, begin a conversation about what they can do differently the next time. What habits were used successfully? What habits need to change? Students will gain motivation when they know processes, practiced daily, lead to improved performances. The key to developing a student's motivation is to underscore the connection between effort, performance, and rewards.

THE HACK IN ACTION

Grace, a high school junior, wanted to audition for the State Honors Choir. She loved singing and saw the State Honors Choir as the pinnacle of musical experience. She dreamed of standing next to the best of her peers, making powerful and moving music.

Since she'd never explored the audition process, she approached her choir director after class. "Could you help me audition for the State Honors Choir?" she asked.

The teacher shuffled papers on the piano. "I don't think you have the voice for it."

Grace hadn't prepared herself to hear this. She didn't know how to respond. She never considered that she wasn't good enough to audition. "Okay, thanks," she said as she turned to leave.

When she got home, Grace told her mom about the conversation.

"Well, I guess you have work to do," her mom said.

Grace was again surprised. Her mom didn't display sympathy. She didn't agree with the teacher or even offer to call her and complain. Instead, Grace's mom pointed to what was next. She asked Grace to focus on improving and to identify what she could address in order to get the outcome she desired.

Grace said, "It felt like my mom gave me permission to take control. To determine what happened next."

Throughout the rest of the year, Grace studied with a private voice teacher. She listened to arias and operas, recordings of ensembles and world-famous groups. She analyzed tonality and sang every day. Grace knew she could put in the work and improve.

At the end of her senior year, Grace auditioned not for the State

Honors Choir but for university music programs. It wasn't the outcome she originally dreamed of—it was better. Grace received a full music scholarship to sing in college.

Today, Grace Bielski teaches choir in Wisconsin. "I want to help my students fall in love with a good process by showing up and working as part of a team," she says.

Grace couldn't have known where that conversation with her high school choir director would lead her, but she's grateful her mom gave her permission to take control. "It feels good to be part of something that's done well. I want my students to trust that if they put in the work, it will pay off," she said.

Outcomes like ACT scores, grade point averages, and test scores emphasize results at the expense of learning. The key is to incentivize habits that lead to growth and to help students understand that efforts lead to rewards and the only thing students can change is the process. Create a how-driven classroom that puts students in control. Allow them to decide what to do, to do the work, to make improvements, to move forward, to make mistakes, to learn from them, and to improve.

When you relinquish control, you allow your students to realize that success starts with a series of failures and that trying and failing is the best way to improve.

PRODUCE POSITIVE COMPETITION
Reframe Comparison

Not everything you put your heart and hands into works out. But not putting all your heart into something is worse than any of that.
— RACHEL WOLCHIN, AUTHOR

THE PROBLEM: Students compare outcomes

THE STUDENTS WHO earn A's on the test feel worthy, while students who earn lesser grades fall to their inclination of comparison. They look at peers who earned top marks and think of themselves as not as smart as those peers or that they'll never achieve those standards.

This comparison hurts our students and forms an internal scorecard. Students trudge through classes as a single player, aiming to out-play, out-wit, or out-work those around them. And this leads to isolation, irritability, self-criticism, and overthinking.

It's miserable to live in constant measurement and self-judgment—and this becomes worse when students pick up their phones and open social media. The comparison fire rages, hot and bright, in a thousand more ways: I'm not smart enough, not pretty enough, not skinny enough, not popular enough, not funny enough.

In the classroom, students' internal scorecards are in play. For example, Addison is motivated by earning academic honors, and Caroline gauges herself against her classmates. These students are not valuing the process of learning or growing; they're just comparing their outcomes. If we look a bit deeper, we'll see that both Addison and Caroline are stuck in a spiral of self-doubt, maybe even self-loathing and self-sabotage. Cheating is rampant in schools for this very reason. Students look at cheating as a way to keep up with those around them; cheating is perceived as a fast and easy way to become a winner and gain an outcome.

Consider what happened during one of my creative writing classes: The students and I watched "Inside a Suicide Prevention Center in Puerto Rico,"—the *New York Times* documentary that author Noel Quiñones used as the inspiration for his original poem.

After we watched the documentary, I passed out a copy of Quiñones's poem, *Permission*. As we read the poem, I asked the students to 1) pay attention to the words Quiñones took from the documentary and 2) underline what they found to be the most important words.

BY FOCUSING ON THE PROCESS, COMPARISON AND COMPETITION CAN MOTIVATE AND ENGAGE STUDENTS.

That's when Addison's hand went up.

"Yes?" I asked.

"Are you collecting this?"

I find this question insufferable, and I've heard it more times than I care to admit. "I want to make sure I'm hearing you correctly, Addison." I tried to speak with sincerity. "Are you saying you're only going to do this if I'm grading it?"

"Yes," he said.

"Addison, let's just look at the poem and not worry about grades. I want you to pay attention to language choices instead, okay?"

I hoped to push Addison to consider what his question suggested: that he didn't care about learning. That he didn't care about the intrinsic value of the assignment. That he didn't care to notice which lines he found important or effective; that he didn't care about the discussion that would follow or what he would or would not contribute to the discussion; that he was disinterested in the process and felt he would not learn anything by doing the exercise.

I wanted Addison to care about learning to the best of his ability and to tackle each task with a positive attitude, open mind, and willingness to work. I wanted him to enjoy the process and learn that if he works through measurable daily habits, good things will follow. I wanted Addison not to worry about grades and assessment but to concern himself with being the best Addison he can be each day.

THE HACK: Produce positive competition

Competition can be negative when there are clear winners and losers, but by turning competition on its head, everyone can win. The key: get students to compare the small things (the process) rather than the large things (the outcomes). By focusing on the process, comparison and competition can motivate and engage students.

In comparing small things, students hone their processes and find new benchmarks for skill sets. They also notice what is or isn't working and what needs to be changed or remain the same. When students compare their processes, they improve themselves and each other.

Reframing comparison is about realizing the work is never done. Even when a student has mastered one small skill, the challenge becomes how to master another small skill at a higher level.

In 2017, Shalane Flanagan did what no American woman had accomplished in forty years: she won the New York City Marathon. In the years prior to her historic win, Flanagan designed and implemented a training and performance model for women runners. It was based on the notion that facing competition daily makes each individual better.

She believed every runner improves when surrounded by the best. She actively recruited the most talented athletes to join her on the

Bowerman Track Club. She yearned for teammates to push her, challenge her, and force the best from her.

The result was a training group comprised of the best of the best. Her squad included America's elite, each running for themselves but also using each other to improve. Every day, Flanagan worked with her competition, knowing she would learn from them. She viewed her teammates' progress as fuel for her own advancement.

Every day at practice, she faced the world's toughest competition, and it made her stronger. She learned new warm-ups, new techniques, and new mental strategies. Integral to Flanagan's model was that teammates cheered for each other. Rather than resent a teammate's win, they celebrated it. Team members came to understand that if one woman could succeed, they could too. What one woman achieved became possible for all. Every success came back to inspire and push the others.

The same can be true in your classroom. Take, for example, choir director Nancy Jorgensen. Every spring, Jorgensen organized small ensembles to perform for a judge at her state music festival. As part of students' preparation, groups performed for peers who critiqued their performances, first emphasizing positive qualities then suggesting areas for improvement. Instead of ensembles competing with each other, ensembles coached each other with the goal to score as many top marks as possible.

Following the critique, each ensemble convened in a practice room for more practice. Jorgensen assigned individuals within the group to coach one musical aspect, such as pitch, rhythm, posture, blend, or balance. All members of the ensemble focused on group, rather than individual, improvement.

This process of peer assessment and then peer leadership yielded top marks with judges. Within the choir, students built relationships, worked toward group goals, and invested in the success of many ensembles. Students practiced a process of trying, soliciting feedback, applying that feedback, and trying again. Students also found joy in the process.

WHAT YOU CAN DO TOMORROW

Comparison can make everyone better if approached in a way that adds value. Rather than comparing outcomes, instead rely on evaluating processes to help students see the benefits of doing an activity and how they can improve.

- **Encourage vulnerability.** Provide a safe space for each student to share; this will build community and help them realize they are not alone. Ask students to share what they're trying for the first time. By sharing this, they're saying out loud that they anticipate mistakes and challenges. Just by naming something as new, scary, or unknown, students give themselves permission to fail, owning that part of a successful process is trial and error and learning from mistakes. They're also opening the door for feedback. Which classmates share this experience? Who has done this before? Who are my resources?

   Students who play video games may be able to explain what they learn by playing the game every day. Of course, they don't win every day— so what do they gain from playing better players? What do they learn from failing in a game?

- **Join forces with your students.** When I coached track, my athletes needed no convincing that I was there to help them and lead them in the right direction. But in the classroom, students don't ask questions, look for insight, or come in with the same goal: to better themselves. When we work with students as part of their team, they are more likely to be vulnerable and to adopt the growth mindset of athletes. How can you collaborate and join your students in what they are working on or learning today? How can you be more of a coach? How can you help them focus on improving or enjoying the process?

In writing classes, for example, consider making a class book of student work or asking students to share work with outside sources, like the school's literary magazine or a writing festival. Student work may also be featured on your classroom bulletin board, in the school newsletter, or on the school's social media pages.

- **Build relationships in class.** Positive relationships allow students to be vulnerable; they also help students reframe comparison. It's not about a classmate being better or worse; it's about the collective working together.

  Consider predictable structures that build community:

  ‣ Conduct a daily meeting.

  ‣ End each class with a whip-around.

  ‣ Use team-building exercises.

  ‣ Encourage students to share what they do outside of school.

  ‣ Pair students with different classmates at different times.

  ‣ Share appropriate details about yourself with your students.

  ‣ Allow time for fun.

A BLUEPRINT FOR FULL IMPLEMENTATION

Comparison and competition are ingrained in our school systems—as well as American culture. An overly competitive environment, or an atmosphere that compares outcomes, steals enjoyment. And what students don't enjoy, they are less likely to return to. To increase investment in the process, reframe comparison and competition in your classroom and build a healthy environment of trust and vulnerability.

Step 1: Flip the narrative.

A growth mindset allows students to see assignments as learning they *get* to do instead of tasks they're forced to trudge through. Present activities as events that build. Spend time explaining why students are completing the work and then give them time to create a positive return. The narrative in your classroom helps students become aware of the benefits of each assignment. It allows them to see each task as achievable through collaboration and community.

Step 2: Outline how to use comparison and competition.

Model how to reframe comparison and competition. Share with students how you use contrast to improve your process. When and how do you notice and explore how others perform? How do you use a community to better your process? How do you gather feedback? Help students understand that comparison can add value if they focus on the processes of daily habits rather than on outcomes.

Step 3: Honor students' interests.

Empower students with choices. Does a student like cars? Do they love making videos? Work with student preferences as much as possible. Let them be their authentic selves. If a student wants to write about cars all semester, let them. This will build an investment, appreciation, and enjoyment for learning and growing. It will also motivate them to work through difficult tasks.

Many of Nancy Jorgensen's Freshmen Boys' Choir students enrolled simply to fulfill their fine arts requirement, showing minimal interest in daily activities. Although Jorgensen could not generate motivation for her students, she could nurture it. For the holiday concert, Jorgensen asked the boys to help choose their repertoire. The class nominated songs, listened to recordings, and then voted on selections. Their chosen song became a favorite to rehearse, and they encouraged each other to audition for the solo parts. After the concert, they listened to the recording, and many expressed pride in their performance. Jorgensen found that when students have a background or interest in a subject, exploring that further will be easier, energize them, and create genuine motivation.

Step 4: Be flexible.

Does a student prefer to type rather than handwrite? Or do they want to use a purple pen? Having control over even the smallest decisions can make a huge difference in motivation. Of course, some restrictions are necessary; they provide a framework or expectation. But too many are debilitating. In my classroom, what's most important is that the students are invested in their writing and that they write every day. I aim to be flexible enough to allow students to find joy in each activity.

Flexibility can be seen in what and when. For example, in an automotive technology class, students bring in cars for repair and choose which projects to tackle. In a manufacturing class, students choose items they want to build and sell.

Step 5: Reframe success.

Get away from unhealthy labeling and remove "right" or "wrong" from your vocabulary. Try referring to answers as "a way to try" or "a way to solve." Ask students to share multiple answers, affirming that there is no "right" or "wrong" but instead multiple ways to approach and solve problems. What different habits could students build? What processes might work? Encourage students to try out the different methods shared.

As teachers, let's stop placing students in the top half or curving. Instead, we can help students recognize processes that may work better than others. We can prompt them to compare behaviors; what changes can they make that lead to better performances? Help them prioritize habits. During classroom activities, consider seating strong students in the middle. They will lead the others. The leaders benefit from gaining respect and building confidence, and the followers benefit from improving their performance.

Step 6: Encourage collaboration.

Allow students to help each other. Consider a "Performance Friday," where students share a win with their classmates. Establish high expectations (in Jorgensen's choir class, she required the piece to be memorized and for the student to have an accompaniment). After each performance, allow time for the student to field comments from peers (Jorgensen asked her students to start with a compliment but also to feature critiques that encouraged specific ways to improve). Although responses begin with a positive, the idea is that each student receives a reaction that can be used to improve. The purpose (the performance or concert) motivates them to practice and prepare, and the feedback pushes the student forward. This concept works well in all content areas, whether students are preparing a physics lab, writing a story, memorizing the table of elements, or sketching a self-portrait.

Step 7: Value done over perfect.

Students fail to complete tasks for a variety of reasons. Some labor over details, some don't want to hand in work unless it's perfect, and others don't try at all because they're afraid to fail. But this is a sticky situation. Aiming for perfection is self-sabotage. Nothing can truly be perfect, and no good comes from doing nothing. This is not to say that students shouldn't value quality. What is done should be done well, but students also need to accept that chasing perfection is wasted energy. They also need time and space to produce positive comparisons. How did students complete tasks? What can they learn from another student's process? How can students fine-tune a learning experience that didn't satisfy them?

Step 8: Evaluate your assessment strategies.

How can you use assessment to build healthy comparison and competition? How can your assessments communicate to students that done is better than perfect?

Consider asking students to hand in their work so far. Don't request a final piece or compare the draft against a rubric. Instead, simply collect the most current version. During a subsequent class, students could share that draft with a peer or the teacher and receive feedback. It doesn't matter that the draft isn't perfect; it is about assessing that work was produced and shared. Likewise, a teacher could assess the comparison. Did the student provide feedback to a classmate? Did they use textual evidence to support their suggestions? Did they take that feedback and compare it against their own current draft?

> **COMPARISON WON'T STEAL JOY IF STUDENTS NOTICE HOW SOMEONE ELSE DID THE WORK, NOT JUST THE RESULT THEY ACHIEVED.**

OVERCOMING PUSHBACK

It's a delicate balance to present boundaries and expectations but also allow for freedom. Too many choices debilitate, but with a bit of direction, your students will take control. They will point their project where they want it to go, they will execute a series of actionable habits, they will compare processes, and, in taking control of their work, they will find joy.

But isn't comparison the thief of joy? Yes, and that's a famous Theodore Roosevelt quote, but not all comparison steals joy. The key is to use someone else's success to push your students and their processes. Comparison won't steal joy if students notice *how* someone else did the work, not just the result they achieved. Think of a concert that features several groups at your school, from entry-level to top-performance groups. Younger students see the top performers in action and strive for the same level of expertise. The students are not comparing themselves but are using the top level as motivation. They also notice how students got to the top: they started at the entry level, practiced daily with a coach, auditioned for select groups, and practiced every day.

I can't get students to change their mindsets. It sounds like it would be impossible, but it helps when your students view you and their classmates as part of their team, not as competitors. At the end of each quarter, I ask my students what they enjoyed working on the most. Students say their favorite assignment was a collaborative piece about nature's wonders. Although this assignment feels like it might be restrictive (they have to write about nature, and they have to work in an intergenerational group), it actually is the opposite. Students can choose their teams (and many invite me, parents or grandparents, siblings, friends, or significant others to join them) and their format (poems, essays, original photos along with their piece). In this project, students have reframed comparison. They are not judging each other but leveraging each person's strengths—celebrating and utilizing each other to collaboratively meet the shared goal. By using comparison in a healthy way, students are not self-centered but self-rewarded.

THE HACK IN ACTION

Beth Schueth co-taught a Global Capstone class that featured several teachers from departments, including social studies, science, language arts, and foreign language. In the class, teachers work collaboratively to help students complete service campaigns to earn the Wisconsin Certificate of Global Competence and improve a global issue. This accomplishment is noted on transcripts and was designed by the Wisconsin Department of Public Instruction "to improve global learning across the curriculum in an effort to prepare all students to be workforce-, world-, and life-ready with global competence."

Schueth said, "Throughout the development of each student's campaign, we're teaching them the tools for making change."

Two students in the class decided to devote their campaign to implementing the United Nations sustainable development goal of quality education.

"I saw how wealth and class can impact an education," one student said. "I care about literacy rates, and I saw a disparity in our county. I wanted to make a change and difference."

The students held a book drive, collecting young readers and children's books. They placed boxes in classrooms, sent emails, and made connections. Then, they personally delivered donated books to cities across the state.

"Getting out of my school and into the community motivates me," one student said. "It takes so much effort, but there is more of a reward knowing someone is getting the books. I set my own standards, and that motivated me. I had to think about what I can achieve, and that made me work harder because I did not want to let myself down."

In Schueth's classroom, all students work together as they study social justice, environmental issues, environmental justice, politics, trade and business, and aesthetics. Classmates learn from each other and are able to assist and motivate progress.

Schueth said, "We're not here to measure success but to note that they did it. The key is passion. When the students choose something they want to change in the world, they're invested in learning the tools necessary to make change."

She asks her students, "What tugs on your heartstrings? How does this affect you?" Her students make connections with the world and note their emotional responses. Then, Schueth gets students to consider what they can do about it. It's not about groups outdoing others but about noticing how groups are successful and helping each group succeed.

"I want to ignite the hands and minds of every student, to get them to make connections, have emotional responses, and to act on their passions," she said.

Outcome-based learning encourages students to measure themselves against classmates, teammates, and siblings. In these comparisons, some students thrive while others tell themselves they're not good enough and they never will be, so why try? On the other hand, sports are a good example of a process-based model. Athletes are invested in the success of others because then the team succeeds. Consider professionals who celebrate each other's successes, like writers when a colleague publishes a book. Many books can and will be published, but another's success is not a threat—it is an example of what is possible. It's also a model for *how* it's possible.

When students compare outcomes, they are less likely to enjoy the process of working and more likely to experience jealousy or poor self-esteem. They are also less likely to improve their processes. Grades and scores are one way students compare themselves, but they also do so in class competitions or rankings. By reframing competition and comparing the process (not the outcome), students will be more likely to gain confidence.

What competitions are built into your classroom? How can you reframe them to increase students' joy and commitment to the process? How can you encourage students to sharpen each other as iron sharpens iron?

DEVELOP THE INNER VOICE
Use Mantras and Self-Talk

Continuous improvement is better than delayed perfection.
— MARK TWAIN, WRITER

THE PROBLEM: Students don't believe in themselves

SOME STUDENTS TELL themselves, "I can't," without even trying. Some hide behind perfectionism, avoiding failure by refusing to try. Some wonder, *What if someone really knew? What if they finally saw that I don't know what I'm doing? That I don't deserve my achievements?* Other students tell themselves they cannot change what happens to them—they were just dealt a bad hand. Fear, self-criticism, and fixed mindsets paralyze students and prevent progress; they keep students from adopting an effective process.

The problem is that students haven't been taught emotional intelligence or mindfulness. In my high school, the choir director recruits top singers to join her advanced music theater troupe. She looks for students with a good sense of pitch, musical sensitivity, and the ability to work in a group, and then she encourages them to audition. Despite her faith in their abilities, some of her most talented students are reluctant to audition for this top ensemble.

Peer pressure in school is powerful, with an unwritten code about which activities are acceptable for boys and which are better for girls. Some students succumb to this pressure and try out for the basketball team when their real talent is in the arts. Then there is the pressure to only participate in popular activities, and some students refuse to be in a group that doesn't attract the school's social elite. Other students won't audition because they fear a public failure. If they don't try, no one will ever know they failed. Because they lack confidence or the strength to follow their interests and desires, these students deny themselves an opportunity to learn, to make good friends, to improve their skills, and to have an enjoyable school experience.

THE HACK: Develop the inner voice

Students have convinced themselves it would take an impossible level of intelligence or skill to write a ten-page research paper, get a part in the school play, or become a varsity swimmer. But it doesn't take an unachievable level of intelligence or skill; it just takes predictable behaviors—a process executed over days and weeks and months.

As teachers, we want our students to see the wonders within themselves and to realize they are the architects of their own growth. To do this, we need to model optimism, hard work, and gratitude. We need to help our students train their inner monologue to be positive and kind and to change "what ifs" to "even ifs"—and from "have to" to "get to."

Back to the choir director recruiting students into an advanced ensemble: One year, a talented tenor refused to audition for a top group, citing a lack of experience. He said he felt intimidated because most of his peers took private voice lessons. Every week, his peers met with voice instructors who helped them with tricky passages, taught them how to breathe, or coached them in foreign languages and diction. This young man's family didn't have the financial means to pay for lessons, which made him feel unworthy of joining the others.

To remedy the situation, the choir director contacted a few donors and a local private voice coach and struck a deal. The donor would fund part of the tenor's weekly lessons, and the voice coach agreed to a reduced fee in return for the tenor doing work on her farm.

The young man took a few lessons, built his confidence, and auditioned for the elite ensemble. He passed the audition and landed in a group where his talents were appreciated. There, he had the opportunity to improve further.

Be attentive to mindsets that inhibit student success. The solutions are not always quick or easy, and sometimes they take time and imagination. Students need our help to build a positive attitude and approach.

The end of the story: the agreement with the scholarship donor and private voice teacher extended for several years and benefited other students too. Although this is only one example, we can find ways to influence the inner monologues within our classrooms.

We all have an internal monologue that impacts our mood, achievement, and stress level. To take on a task, students must first believe they are likely to succeed. Once they believe they can, they will invest in the process. Encouraging students to believe they possess the skills is the first part of the prescription to overcoming anxiety, fear, or doubt.

One easy way to develop positive self-talk is to say mantras. Mantras build a growth mindset, increase optimism, and help students produce, especially in moments of doubt. Mantras have been shown to relax and focus the brain. Mantras can also be used to foster relationships with students and build students' skills.

Entrepreneur Bethenny Frankel ends her podcast by asking guests about their mantras. Frankel has several: "Come from a place of yes," "Pros play hurt," and "If you can't run with the big dogs, stay chained to the porch."

Olympic silver medalist Courtney Frerichs believes mantras built her confidence and led her to success in Tokyo. Frerichs heard her coaches use mantras. One coach, Joe Franklin, said, "Expect nothing. Achieve everything." Another coach, Jerry Schumacher, said, "Let yourself run." Taking inspiration from a longer quote, "Be fearless in the pursuit of what sets your soul on fire," Frerichs used one word as her mantra: "Fearless."

Peloton instructor Christine D'Ercole says, "I am, I can, I will, I do."

Amanda Gorman, the 2020 inaugural poet, has this mantra: "I am the daughter of Black writers who are descended from Freedom Fighters who broke their chains and changed the world. They call me." Gorman repeats her mantra before giving speeches or reciting poems because she says it gives her strength and courage.

In addition to mantras, consider memoirs. Larry Smith created six-word memoirs, asking people to share their life story in six words. Since Smith's original challenge, six-word memoirs have expanded into books and a website that provides classroom features, contests, and lesson plans.

Six-word memoirs can fit in even the most crammed curriculum. Teachers can use six-word memoirs as an icebreaker. They can even be framed as a student's mantra—as a refrain they can repeat in difficult times to remind themselves who they are or who they want to be. Student mantras or six-word memoirs can also decorate your classroom walls. Image 5.1 shows student six-word memoirs posted in Terri Carnell's high school classroom. Image 5.2 shows a sample of student six-word memoirs published by my students.

Image 5.1

A SAMPLE OF STUDENTS' SIX-WORD MEMOIRS
created during the pandemic:

Coronavirus, bad, but worse we've had.
Coming together is the solution.
Took things for granted: never again.
Adventure creates curiosity; curiosity cures boredom.
Embracing my fears and my imperfections.
During hard times, we create masterpieces.
Toilet paper's gone, but hope isn't.

Image 5.2

WHAT YOU CAN DO TOMORROW

Mantras allow students to believe a successful process is possible; mantras verbalize feelings and grant ownership over habits.

- **Share mantras with your students.** Allow students to see successful people use mantras to frame their outlook. You can use the ones mentioned earlier or conduct an internet search for mantras from other leaders. Ask students to share times when they used mantras. During a sports event, did they hear their coach say, "Get after it" or "You've got this" or "Dig deep" or "Look ahead" or "Enjoy it"? Some athletes will tell themselves, "Two more steps," when they think they can't go any further.

- **Ask students to create a mantra.** A mantra will encourage students to act, or it will give students something to believe in. A mantra is a personal mission statement that helps move students forward on difficult days. Podcaster and athlete Carrie Tollefson said, "The reason I use word cues is I just want to have a positive thought or a productive thought going on. If there's a negative thought, I can squash it right away."

In creating a mantra, students can consider taking inspiration from a quote. Ideas can also be found in book characters, role models, movies, or video game characters. See Image 5.3 for a list of student-generated mantras.

One of my former students, Marleh Lehmann, was tragically killed in a car accident a few years after graduation. After Lehmann died, her sister launched a clothing brand named after her sister's motto: "No worries. None." The brand sells worldwide and uses proceeds to fund scholarships. Consider asking students what they want their legacy to be. Lehmann had "No worries. None." tattooed on her body. What would students choose as their tattoo?

STUDENT-GENERATED MANTRAS:

I have hot sauce in my veins.	Just get through today.
Have honor.	One step at a time.
Work smarter, not harder.	Positive thoughts make positive energy.
Now, not later.	What you do comes back to you.
Don't think, just do.	Words fail, actions prevail.
Just breathe through it.	Stay soft.
To whatever end.	There's no I in team, but there is me.
Just got to get through this.	Again, next one.
You owe it to yourself.	Work for what you want, enjoy it once you have it.
Everything is temporary.	There is always another chance.
Just send it.	Don't think, just do.
Someone's got it worse.	Strive for perfection, attain excellence.
It is what it is.	Just keep trying.
You find perfection in repetition.	Never be okay with just being okay.
Every day is a fresh start.	Fear is to be defeated before you even try.
Do your best.	You got this.
Ignorant minds start and feed fires.	Cover the footsteps of the greats before you.
The best revenge is massive success.	

Image 5.3

- **Ask students to create a metaphor about themselves.** These metaphors are mantras. Students could reference professional examples, including "I am" poems or *The Delight Song of Tsoai-talee* by N. Scott Momaday. See Image 5.4 for a student poem example.

I AM THE WEATHER
by Alicia Bouton

Everchanging without any thought,
one second I'm raining, the other not

I blast the fields with wind and showers,
to heal the thirsty cries from the flowers

I cover the world in a blanket of snow,
then send out the sun when noses start to blow

Men of weather like to try to predict,
but I remember I may change and on you,

may I play a little trick.

Image 5.4: A student poem inspired by *The Delight Song of Tsoai-talee* by N. Scott Momaday.

Student Dalton Hribar wrote the poem "I AM Unique" (read it in Appendix F) and had this to say about the poem and the experience:

> "One of my all-time favorite pieces of writing in high school was my I AM Unique poem. I better learned who I am, and got to know myself more. I developed an understanding of who I am, and what makes me unique.
>
> In my I AM Unique poem, I discovered what I am not, and what makes me different from others. I am always finding ways to get involved and stay involved. I am

always doing something and don't have a lot of time for fun. I see there is beauty in everyone and everything; to me, nothing is disgusting; we all are brilliant in our own way. I discovered that I really do not have enemies or people I dislike. Yes at times I may feel angry with others, but I never let that get to me or let that change my view of the person. I try to be kind to everyone no matter who they are, no matter their race, religion, gender, views ...

I really have developed my set of values and morals throughout high school. I found the value of integrity and just doing the right thing even when no one is watching. I have grown in my leadership. I believe I have the power to change the world for the better and become a better leader. My leadership has grown astronomically throughout high school, especially this last year and semester. My words and actions can make this place better. The small things I do can have the largest impacts on others.

OUR STUDENTS ARE OUTSIDE THEIR COMFORT ZONES THROUGHOUT THE SCHOOL DAY AS THEY ARE CONSTANTLY PRESENTED WITH NEW CONTENT AND STRESSFUL SITUATIONS.

My I AM Unique poem was one of my favorite pieces of writing this semester, and I feel that this poem helped me reflect and discover who I am, who I am not, and how I am unique. This poem really summarizes my high school journey of developing my character, personality, and identity."

A BLUEPRINT FOR FULL IMPLEMENTATION

The first step to action is a thought—a belief that whatever one chases is possible. To build belief, use mantras to remind students to show up every day and work the process.

Step 1: Ask students to write a mantra from a different perspective.

Kelly Gallagher, teacher and coach, suggests this activity: Ask students to give advice from the perspective of something else—maybe a pet, body of water, or a favorite artist. Consider, for example, what the mantra of a tree would be. Gallagher posted an infographic to his Twitter account with this advice from a tree: "Stand tall and go proud. Go out on a limb. Reach for the sky. Adapt to change. Branch out. Stay grounded. Remember your roots. Drink plenty of water. Get rid of dead wood. Be confident. Never stop growing. Bend before you break. Turn over a new leaf. Enjoy the view."

Step 2: Strengthen community and connections.

For the most part, our students are outside their comfort zones throughout the school day as they are constantly presented with new content and stressful situations. They are scared and in unfamiliar territory as they learn trigonometry, scales, or the stock market. Remind students that they are not expected to be good right away or have it all figured out. What they are expected to be is open, willing to learn and try, and aware of their thoughts, feelings, and actions. Model this for your students as you ask for help and are vulnerable, and share when you are wrong. Allow your students to see you try new things and fail. Help students understand that when they talk about things, they get easier.

Throughout your course, continue to strengthen your classroom community. What do your students, together, want to accomplish? What do they want to create? How can they get there together?

Step 3: Build awareness.

Everyone has doubts. Make that realization public in your classroom. Ask students to reflect on a time when they felt undeserving. Just revisiting how they overcame will remind students that they had the power to continue their processes.

In discussions or journal entries, ask your students to explore when they've felt unworthy. Encourage them to write (or talk) about times when they didn't fit in. This generates individual awareness, which will ultimately lead to better classroom awareness and the tools to manage doubt. How can you help students realize the only thing they can control is their reaction?

Ask students to share their feelings. Sharing how they feel gives them ownership. It will also help them accept that everyone feels the same way. "How prepared do you feel for the concert?" "How are you doing today?" This may be as simple as a thumbs-up, thumbs-neutral, or thumbs-down response. On tasks or assignments, build awareness by asking students to check red, yellow, or green boxes. Or by adding a short question to assignments, asking students to reflect on their preparation, habits, or feelings.

Step 4: Visually remind students of your values.

Signage, posters, and bulletin boards make your values visible. Survey your classroom space. What messages do your visuals convey? A welcoming and safe classroom community will remind students they are not alone in their thoughts or feelings.

The images in Rick Witte's classroom reflect what students do every day. One sign hangs outside of Witte's

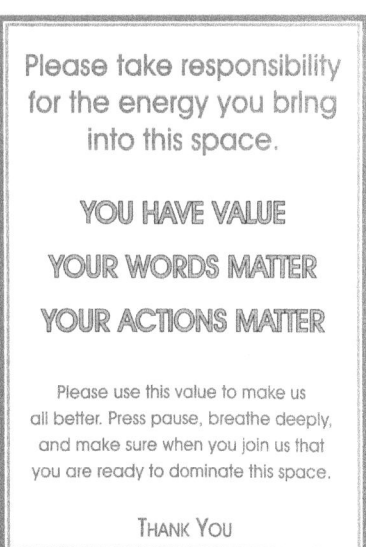

Image 5.5

door, and students hit the sign on the way in. It's each student's choice to hit the sign, but students collectively decide to do it. The sound is affirming; it's an auditory reminder of the classroom's values. See a couple of Witte's signs in Images 5.5 and 5.6.

Image 5.6

Nancy Jorgensen painted a map of the United States on her classroom wall. Every time her group of musicians traveled to a city, they added a silver star. The visual confirmation celebrated group progress and individual achievement.

Consider displaying a calendar of the semester with all the curriculum goals and projects students will accomplish. Take students to your auditorium or field house. Show them the Hall of Fame to remind them of what has been possible in their school. When students see banners in the gym, they are reminded that the school values fitness and productive competition, as well as wins and championships. You might also ask students to research or learn about the fields or stadiums named after heroes. Who are these heroes? What do people admire about them? Schools also have scholarships named after people. Consider making a list and talking about who these heroes are.

Step 5: Craft a class mantra.

Mantras trigger student behavior. Using a class mantra creates predictability and emphasizes what is important in your classroom.

Witte uses these phrases: "What have you done for someone else today?" and "Press pause." Ask students to share the phrases they hear other teachers repeat. What do those mantras suggest about what those teachers value? Then, ask students to collaboratively craft a class mantra. In creating this mantra, students decide together what they want to focus on. For example:

- "You are a singer. Take that responsibility seriously."
- "Get after it!"
- "Done is better than perfect."
- "Everything depends on work."

Step 6: Ask students to create a vision board.

To believe what they want is possible, students need to see it. Plenty of evidence shows that manifestation can work. In the book *The Secret*, Rhonda Byrne describes how we can, by the law of attraction, draw in experiences we desire. Vision boards are a way for students to focus on what they want. A vision board:

- sets out a future that students can see
- helps students believe what they want is possible
- works as a goal-setting mechanism

MANTRAS ARE ONE WAY YOU CAN HELP STUDENTS DEVELOP A HEALTHY INNER VOICE.

Encourage students to place their vision boards where they will see them. Suggest hanging the boards inside the locker, on a class binder, or on a bedroom wall. Remind students to modify the vision board; it is a living artifact that should change as their vision changes. Image 5.7 shows Gwen Jorgensen's vision board that I share with students.

Image 5.7

OVERCOMING PUSHBACK

Each student's process will be filled with mistakes and imperfections, but students' responses to those challenges are what determine their performance. Here are common negative statements about mantras and mindsets, along with suggested responses.

Mantras are hokey. They can be, but if you find one you truly believe in, it will work. Whatever your mantra, own it. If you're faking it, students will see right through it (and you) and reward you with eye rolls or laughs.

In writing this book, I kept repeating this mantra: "Just a little today; a little more; that's all." This mantra allowed me to reframe my situation (that often felt impossible) and refocus on what I could control (my process). I didn't find my mantra hokey; I truly believed it, and it helped propel me forward.

I can't change a student's mindset. Your students likely have never understood that they can control their thoughts and redirect their emotions. Building a growth mindset will take time and practice. Bring awareness to the power students have over their thoughts so they can shift their mindsets. Small, incremental changes are sustainable. Be patient and remember that students will gain strength and insights from your focus on positive thinking and emotional intelligence. Model the behaviors you want to see in them. See Image 5.8 for ideas.

TO HELP STUDENTS BUILD EMOTIONAL INTELLIGENCE AND RESILIENCE, SHOW THEM HOW TO:

- manage impulses
- own responsibility
- listen, think, and communicate
- adapt
- apply knowledge
- find enjoyment
- remain open
- persist

Image 5.8

I'm not a counselor, and this is too much emotional stuff. Your students need help developing emotional intelligence. Mantras are one way you can help students develop a healthy inner voice. Your students will not work if they aren't invested, and if students aren't emotionally ready to handle the content, then they will essentially fail before they even begin. If mantras aren't your thing, find other ways to help students train their inner voice to be resilient.

THE HACK IN ACTION

The language we use matters, especially in times of stress. In a *Journal of Personality and Social Psychology* article titled "Self-Talk as a Regulatory Mechanism: How You Do It Matters," researchers showed the value of adding one's own name within a mantra.

Choral director Grace Bielski illustrated this concept when she wanted her students to sing "Lift Every Voice and Sing" like they meant it, like they believed it. But her sophomore South Select Choir sounded more like shadows, whispering when they needed to belt.

"I had an intervention," Bielski said. "I knew something had to change in order for my students to believe the lyrics."

Bielski started by inviting sections of students (sopranos and altos) to the hallway. She asked the students to form a circle so they could see each other. Then, she asked them to repeat: "I am a good singer."

Like they sang, the students quietly repeated the mantra, almost in a whisper.

"I am a good singer."

"I am a good singer."

"I am a good singer."

Bielski said, "I told the girls that this was their subconscious laying out what their life will be. In order to change the narrative, I told them they have to believe and to buy in. They had to say they were a singer louder."

On the next attempt, her students repeated the mantra with a bit more volume, but they still didn't sound like they believed they were good singers.

"I thought if I got them to bring themselves into the mantra, that might work, so then I asked them to use their name along with 'I am a good singer,'" Bielski said. The next time around the circle, each girl said, "I am (insert name), and I am a good singer."

As each girl said it, Bielski said she felt the students gain courage. The sopranos and altos increased their volume.

"I wanted them to believe they were good enough to sing the lyrics—that every voice needed to be lifted and sung."

Bielski used this mantra for the days leading up to the concert to remind students of their responsibility. The mantras slowly became her students' thoughts, which directly impacted their feelings, which in turn, affected their actions.

By using mantras as a behavior and part of the process, Bielski helped improve her students' confidence. She found that mantras reduced students' doubts and ruminating thoughts, helped change their inner monologue, disrupted their impostor syndrome, and allowed her students to believe they were good singers.

As author and speaker Luvvie Ajayi Jones said, "Impostor syndrome in the beginning might be 'I can't do this.' Then, 'I'm not ready for this.' Then it can become, 'I need to continue to earn my greatness.'"

Be aware of "impostor syndrome" roadblocks in students' lives. Work to build their positive inner monologue through signage, vision boards, research, discussions, and mantras. A strong inner voice will scaffold students through difficult tasks and help them work through the process in manageable chunks as they think more deeply about their work, organize their thoughts, set their goals, and develop a plan to meet those goals.

GENERATE FEEDBACK LOOPS
Analyze, Revise, and Improve

Grading does not improve learning, in the same way
a scale does not cause someone to lose weight.
— Tom Schimmer, author and speaker

THE PROBLEM: Grades are terrible feedback

WE'VE WATCHED THIS scene unfold in our classrooms: students receive a graded assignment with the teacher's marks in the column, noting errors or commendations. Students flip past these comments to the back page. When the student finds the score, they shove the assignment into their backpack. Or dump it into the trash can. They received the grade, so the learning stops; there is nothing else for them to do.

Grades present so many problems, including:

- Grades are outcomes.

- Grades stall progress.

- Grades prevent risk-taking.

- Grades provide no opportunity for improvement.

- Grades are one-way streets.

- Grades are not tools for learning.

In high school, when athletes don't perform well in an event, they often badger the coach for help. Athletes' reactions are intuitive—when faced with a problem, they look for feedback with the intent to incorporate it. What can they eat to make them stronger? What can they do to build endurance? How can they improve their stroke? When can they schedule extra laps? The problem is that students rarely seek out or implement this kind of feedback in the classroom.

We want students to receive and to give feedback. Students need to know what is working and what isn't, and feedback helps students identify behaviors to continue or modify.

THE HACK: Generate feedback loops

Generating feedback loops is an essential part of process-based assessment, just like encouraging practice instead of perfection, relinquishing control, producing positive competition, and developing the inner voice. Instead of assessing through grades or criticism, assess through feedback. It is best when given in real time, either verbally or in writing. If it must be shared later, consider recording observations using voice apps or videos so students can hear the tone.

Feedback sources can include:

- formal or informal teacher input on activities, papers, presentations, assignments, tests, homework, projects, and discussions

- students' input to each other

- students' self-assessments

- input from mentors, parents, or outside sources such as competitions, publications, or the public

Effective feedback:

- is evaluative rather than judgmental

- makes students feel better, not bitter

- can be taken seriously, not personally

- stimulates dialogue, discussion, or follow-up

- helps students understand how close they are to the goal

- helps students understand what they need to do to meet the goal

- inspires learning and modification

- illuminates areas of strength and areas to improve

- puts students in control of assessing themselves, their work, and their process

Consider using experiences from your life to emphasize feedback's usefulness. For example, my dad showed my mom a project he was working on—a cheese board with wooden pieces, where the colors created an optical illusion. Except, he flubbed the pattern and couldn't figure out how to fix it. My mom recognized his design from a quilt pattern. She helped him sort the colors into the right order. And it was a good thing: he was almost ready to glue it together with a slew of errors.

Although my mom is a retired choir teacher, she dabbles in writing. She drafts pieces and then brings them to me for feedback. We talk about her writing, and I point out where I'm confused; I ask her questions, and I give suggestions. My mom takes these same pieces to a writing group that includes a cohort of writers from young professionals to retirees like herself. She works through several rounds of advice and drafts before submitting the work to journals. She knows there are no right or wrong suggestions, and she appreciates receiving contradicting opinions. She's gathering responses to her work, developing her skills, and making updates.

We want students to do the same and frame feedback as neutral. Help students view setbacks as opportunities for growth. The goal is for students to make their processes more successful, to engage with reactions in order to improve, and to create and practice sustainable habits. Each student is at a different place and will benefit differently from feedback. Being a successful practitioner is about nuance. Feedback should follow suit and be multilayered, diverse, and incremental. Think of feedback as the way you differentiate and personalize your instruction and assessment.

Feedback can encourage students to continue on the same path or to change direction. You want to help students understand that they can make a change instead of making an excuse. The best feedback:

- uses specific details (avoid "nice" or "good job" or "wow")

- helps students understand why something works or doesn't

- suggests research methods

- makes connections from the student's work to something else

- asks questions that encourage reflection

According to Douglas Stone and Sheila Heen, authors of *Thanks for the Feedback*, there are three types of feedback: gratitude, coaching, and evaluation. Use each of these for different situations. Sometimes students need to know their effort or performance is recognized (gratitude); sometimes they need assistance (coaching); and at other times, they need to know where they stand against the goal (evaluation).

As students practice habits and develop skills, allow for multiple approaches and be timely and specific with your feedback. Afford students the chance to think about changes, and offer confirmation when they move in a constructive direction.

Before students perform, provide opportunities to receive input from a variety of sources. A few weeks before the state music competition, a choir director hired a respected music educator to serve as a clinician. The clinician listened to each madrigal, barbershop, and soloist. After the performances, the clinician provided assessments, including demonstrations of skills. The clinician helped students recognize areas that needed improvement (intonation, rhythmic accuracy, and tone quality) and processes that could assist (imagining the pitch, thinking high, listening, clapping rhythms, and blending).

EACH DAY REQUIRES A DIFFERENT EFFORT FROM YOU AND YOUR STUDENTS. CONTINUALLY IDENTIFY WHAT IS WORKING AND WHAT ISN'T.

Students used the clinician's feedback in the weeks leading up to the competition to improve their execution. Because students performed and received feedback in a group setting, others also identified common setbacks and areas of strength. Students said they appreciated learning new techniques (like tongue-twisters and warm-up chants) and hearing what their classmates executed successfully (diction, engaging an audience, and facial expressions). They also valued a professional's feedback prior to the state event.

Examine how you can give observations that will help students recognize their habits and processes, see how their determination affected their performance, and realize how their effort mattered. You may consider bringing in others, like a clinician, or allowing students to give feedback to each other. Students may also give themselves feedback that will help analyze how their habits and processes were fruitful. When students critique themselves, guide them to map out their processes in order to recognize that success is the result of controllable habits.

Examine the amount of information students receive. Too much is overwhelming. When students see only a few comments they need to address, they feel like the feedback is manageable. They may say to themselves:

- I know what I can do to make this section better.

- This is my best work.

- I'm on the right track.

As the teacher, focus on complimenting effort instead of achievement. Consider:

- "It looks like you're trying to use [specific skill] here. Can you use [that same skill] in other places?"

- "I see you implemented [a technique]. Where else can [this technique] be useful?"

- "You've worked hard on [a specific process]. This allows me to [specific effect]."

After students receive feedback, provide in-class time for them to make changes. You might consider assessing how or if students applied the feedback they've received. Examine your delivery medium. Do your students respond better to verbal feedback? Are they ready to handle it in a whole-class setting? Do they respond better to peers or themselves?

Finally, review your audience and the timing of your feedback. Throughout the year or semester, students' needs change. To generate awareness of and create movement in student work, circle back to nuance. Each day requires a different effort from you and your students. Continually identify what is working and what isn't. Be attuned to your students' needs. Observe conversations, body language, facial expressions, and emotions. You can skim a random sampling of student work, poll students (in-person using thumbs-up, neutral, or sideways or electronically through an app), or collect exit slips.

If you know a student is dealing with a breakup or grieving a grandparent, tread delicately with constructive feedback. Honor students' efforts, especially in trying times. Recognize their resolve and resilience and remember how students deal with feedback: personally. Then, help students accept it as a data point and not as a critique of themselves.

One of my students said:

> "One of the most helpful things about this class was your feedback. You always told me exactly what I did wrong on my pieces and gave me enough feedback to allow me to fix my mistakes and learn from them. However, it's not like you just flat out edited my piece and changed it yourself. I felt like you never just gave me what I was supposed to change, you would instead suggest a different direction. This is perfect for my learning because I feel like some teachers don't give you enough information to learn from your mistakes and just expect you to somehow know what you did wrong."

WHAT YOU CAN DO TOMORROW

Although teachers are accustomed to assessing at the end of a unit or project, it's more effective to provide immediate and daily feedback. Feedback can be informal or formal and is most effective when it gives students the opportunity to find their own mistakes, make purposeful choices, improve, and modify their processes to meet their goals.

- **Shift your mindset from grader to coach.** Gwen Jorgensen, as a high school senior, wanted to work on her stroke mechanics. During practices, her coach recorded an underwater video. After, he showed it to her, pointing out places where she could try different techniques. The purpose was to gather feedback on her performance well before the state meet. What was she doing right? What did she need to work on?

  A coach watches athletes at practice and studies film post-games to improve the team's performance. Coach—instead of grade—your students, and they will begin to see you as their biggest cheerleader and supporter. Build community, a team mentality, and inspire collaboration. Frequently check in. Help students see you advocate for their success. Allow them to practice and scaffold experiences. Work with your students and allow them to work together. Provide class time for students to give each other feedback, which helps create a teamwork mentality.

- **Model the process.** Students often struggle to give and receive effective and constructive feedback. Many students won't want to hurt someone's feelings, or they genuinely don't know what to say. Show students diplomatic tactics.

  Sometimes, I ask a student to work with me on a piece of writing in front of the class. I project a sample of my work and read it out loud. Then, I ask for the editor's reaction. When the student gives me feedback, I present follow-up questions and engage in a dialogue. I rephrase the feedback I'm given, such as: "What I hear you saying is ..." and "Am I understanding you correctly?". This allows the class to see me working through receiving, paraphrasing, and accepting feedback in a neutral way.

After modeling a feedback loop in front of the class, I ask students to journal on what they noticed about the process. As a class, we discuss what each student would have said and how they thought the loop could have improved. After this discussion, I share my plan to work with the feedback I received. I also present questions I want to ask my editor.

You might also share stories from your personal life. For example, my dad makes pallet clocks for family and friends. At each step in his process, he asks for feedback from the recipient. The first choice is about the wood: dark or light? Thick or thin? Rustic or refined? He offers a suggestion and then listens to the recipient's preferences. Once wooden slats are assembled and cut into a forty-four-inch circle, it's time for the numbers. Roman numerals or Arabic? Large or small? Black or white? Again, he offers his vision but decides based on feedback. Finally, he either leaves the wood natural or applies a finish that could be glossy or matte. My dad's goal is to make a clock that is accurate and visually appealing. He understands not everyone has the same aesthetic, and his goal is not just to produce a product but to hone his skills in both woodworking and listening to his customer. (See Image 6.1 to see various pallet clock options.) A feedback loop is crucial for his success.

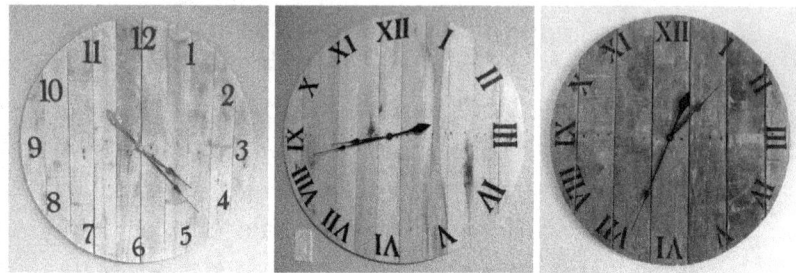

Image 6.1

- **Practice soft skills.** Learning requires engaging with feedback to make constructive changes. Identify what's holding students back and build soft skills to help them move forward. Here are ideas you might consider for mini-lessons:
    ‣ working collaboratively
    ‣ managing time
    ‣ making and implementing plans
    ‣ meeting deadlines
    ‣ thinking creatively
    ‣ persevering
    ‣ asking questions
    ‣ resolving conflicts
    ‣ advocating
    ‣ listening

What activities would help your students practice soft skills? At my high school, students in a special education program run a café. During the Thanksgiving season, they make and sell pies. Orders are placed and fulfilled the week of Thanksgiving. Students learn to work together, manage orders, meet deadlines, and be creative with marketing. Students also receive responses from customers. Which pies were most popular? What can the students do to improve and expedite next year's process?

A BLUEPRINT FOR FULL IMPLEMENTATION

Give students control over how, when, and where they receive feedback; this helps them know you care about them individually and as a whole class.

Step 1: Recognize where students are.

Understanding each student academically and personally requires acute awareness. It is not fair or accurate for us to label students as advanced or struggling; instead, students are where they are. Build a classroom that focuses on one community or team working together. Engage in productive conversations. Create mutual understanding. If you make a mistake, own it and move forward. Encourage students to do the same. Find ways to show students you care. (See the ideas in Image 6.2.)

WAYS TO SHOW STUDENTS YOU CARE:

Assume students try their best.

Have authentic conversations.

Help students understand you want them to learn.

Give each student time.

Admit you don't have all the answers.

Engage in robust discussions.

Say yes more.

Ask questions that prompt genuine responses.

Invest in what your students are interested in.

Ask follow-up questions.

Listen.

Image 6.2

Step 2: Ask students to self-assess their strengths and weaknesses.

Allow students to set their criteria for success and then to use self-analysis to determine their process. Consider asking students to score themselves on a scale of zero to ten. Students will rarely say zero or ten. Then, they have the opportunity to explain how they can get closer to the goal (ten). What habits do they need to implement? What feedback can help them improve? Each student's self-assessment could be recorded in the gradebook as a zero weight. This will communicate progress but not harm the student's overall grade.

You might also consider using a process-based rubric. When students practice giving a presentation, they could use a rubric to note if they used eye contact, engaged in personal interactions, gathered feedback, looked professional, and practiced proper posture. Scoring this with a zero weight can encourage students to practice and improve.

Step 3: Increase effort-focused, positive comments on student work.

Be specific and praise students' efforts. Instead of vague comments like "I'm proud of you," consider:

- "I notice you didn't give up, even when you were challenged by …"
- "I saw the effort you displayed when you …"
- "You found an innovative way to solve this problem when you …"

Effort-based praise helps students recognize that they control their processes and can construct performances they are proud of.

Step 4: Pose questions to increase students' metacognition.

Questions allow you to understand each student's process as well as remind students you are in this with them. See Image 6.3 for the types of questions that encourage updates or modifications. (For in-depth ideas about how to create a culture of inquiry in your classroom, check out Connie Hamilton's book *Hacking Questions*.)

TYPES OF QUESTIONS THAT ENCOURAGE UPDATES OR MODIFICATIONS:

What about ...?

Why did you ...?

What could you do to ...?

What other options are there for ...?

What did you intend for ...?

How did you ...?

Where are you struggling?

Where can I assist?

What habits do you want to implement?

What feedback would you find useful?

What do you want to work on?

Where are you confused?

Image 6.3

Step 5: Use loops.

A loop is a conversation that continues with dialogue and questions. A loop puts all parties in control. At any time, one person can say stop or ask for more feedback. There may be times for vertical feedback (top-down) and horizontal feedback (peer-to-peer); however, the most effective feedback requires each party to engage, invest, analyze, and reflect.

Use teacher-student and student-student loops to build feedback-rich classrooms. In a student-student loop, start small. Ask students to identify the most successful area and explain why. Or ask each student to state what they're struggling with and why. Build in time for discussion. As students converse, feel free to moderate and interject. If certain students need more help, lead them with effort-focused encouragement or questions. Elevate the loop by contributing your questions or asking students to share when they're stuck or don't know what to say.

Step 6: Use indicators to monitor progress.

Prior to giving feedback, identify how much progress each student should make. Tracking progress allows you to know when students are ready for feedback. Consider asking students to give a thumbs-up, thumbs-neutral, or thumbs-down to quickly assess how they feel about their progress. Or use this method to indicate if they are ready for more feedback.

NOTICE THE DIFFERENCE BETWEEN "WHAT CAN I ASSIST YOU WITH?" AND "IS THERE ANYTHING I CAN ASSIST YOU WITH?"

Construct systems that empower students to ask for and implement feedback. In the gradebook, you could note when students seek out feedback. You could also set and assess a goal. For example, communicate that you expect each student to ask for feedback four times during the unit.

Step 7: Dialogue honestly.

Discuss the subjectivity of feedback. To help students understand, ask them to share their favorite songs, bands, music, directors, artists, actors, or writers. Students can talk about different genres and explore different affinities. This doesn't mean one is right or wrong. They are part of a diverse world of varying opinions, and one is not better than another. Feedback is simply a neutral data point they can use to make changes or updates.

When you and your students dialogue honestly about work, consider using "I notice …" statements or asking, "What can I assist you with?"

Notice the difference between "What can I assist you with?" and "Is there anything I can assist you with?" If given a yes-or-no question, students often choose the path of least resistance.

Step 8: As you're giving students feedback, solicit feedback.

Student surveys are a tool to help you grow alongside your students. The more often you gather and use this data, the more successful you can be. This process also allows students to see that you're doing the same thing they are: using feedback to improve. See Image 6.4 for a sample list of statements students can answer on a sliding scale (always, sometimes, never) as a way to provide feedback to the teacher.

STATEMENTS STUDENTS CAN ANSWER ON A SLIDING SCALE (ALWAYS, SOMETIMES, NEVER) TO GIVE THE TEACHER FEEDBACK:

My teacher provides immediate feedback I use to improve my work.

I have opportunities to provide my classmates with feedback.

I have opportunities to address feedback and make updates during class.

My classmates have opportunities to give me feedback.

My teacher helps me gain skills that improve my work.

My teacher understands my goals and how to use feedback to help me reach them.

I receive positive feedback.

I hear my teacher praise my classmates.

I hear my teacher praise my classmates and me equally.

Image 6.4

OVERCOMING PUSHBACK

Grades function ineffectively, as they are subjective judgment or evaluation, not coaching. Instead of grading, focus on feedback that allows students to enjoy and improve the substance of their work.

There's not enough time to give all my students feedback. There will never be enough time, so limit comments and focus on one or two criteria. Narrow comments to your course's guiding principles or to a particular assignment's focal point. This makes providing feedback more manageable. Consider putting students in control. Ask where they need assistance or what they're struggling with. Allow them to determine when or where they want feedback. This builds a student's resolve to engage with useful feedback; it also helps you narrow responses.

Penny Kittle is an author, teacher, and advocate. Kittle spent twenty-one years teaching in a high school and now teaches at the university level. When her students write essays, she uses a common list of criteria. She asks the students to "read these and look at your draft. … Are these reminders, questions, things true about the piece you've given me?" She says, "I cannot write all of this on every draft, or I'd never get back to you … so these are reminders for all of you."

Kittle also asks students to staple an updated draft to the first draft with endnotes. As for the endnotes, she asks students to "explain how you used the research you found … did class notes help you? How? If not, why not? Review all of the criteria and give yourself a holistic grade." Kittle tells students that endnotes show the process behind their draft. Like Kittle, can you provide the class with a list of common comments? Can you ask students to self-assess?

Questions don't work when there is a right or wrong answer. Stay away from questions with right or wrong answers. For example, if a student is using the em dash incorrectly, you don't need to ask a question, as it will come off as condescending or trite. If the student makes an error, just point it out and provide them with the instruction they need to correct it. Questions work best when applied to how students approach a problem or how they can improve their processes.

But I have to give a grade. Most schools require students to receive a grade at several points throughout the semester, but there are ways you can assign grades in a process-based assessment model. Checks, daily points, fair share grading, pass/fail, self-assessment, portfolios, self-grading, and contract grading can all be used to assess a student's process. You can find creative ways to overcome the constraints of traditional grades. Although a grade must be given at some point, focus on implementing a system that allows students to value feedback instead of the grade.

THE HACK IN ACTION

Allison and her classmates are working on poems. In developing ideas, I ask students to consider what story they want to tell, who the character(s) will be, the plot, and the purpose for their poem. After students brainstorm, each one has the opportunity to share ideas verbally with the class. This allows each student to hear thirty ideas. While each student shares, they also receive feedback from peers and me early in the writing process.

As we go around the room and hear ideas, Allison says, "My characters will be my grandma and me. The plot is about how I used to give her dandelions. The twist will be that she actually died. Why I want to write about this: It's important to me because it's the only thing I remember doing with her."

I find Allison's reason for her poem particularly compelling. I say, "I can relate to your topic. I also used to collect dandelions to give to people when I was a child. It sounds like you share a special bond with your family. Your poem would be a wonderful tribute to what your grandma meant to you."

Allison works during a forty-minute class period and submits her first poem draft electronically:

> My yellow, dandelions in a field. I give them to her.
> I gather more to make a bouquet, for grandma,
> I hand them to her but she can't reach. So I lay them on a stone.

In my first round of feedback, I aim to stimulate progress. I've found compliments and praise help students tackle constructive feedback that will come later.

To Allison, I write, "You have a great poem! You're telling a story, it's emotional, and you successfully use the present tense."

I then move to offering feedback line by line:

- "What are you considering for a title?"

- "In the first line, I notice you're missing a verb."

- "I'm wondering about the pronoun 'her' in the first line; did you want to introduce both characters in the first line? Who will your reader think the 'her' refers to?"

- Because students are writing a Korean form of poetry called sijo, Allison needs to use a particular structure. I ask, "How can you make the second line fit more closely to the sijo structure? Remember, each line needs to have between fourteen and sixteen syllables."

After looking at my feedback, Allison uses another forty-minute class period to make updates. She includes her notes and words she's debating with the strike-through feature on her document. This helps me see her writing process.

~~I give her yellow dandelions from the field.~~
I gather ~~more~~ yellow dandelions to make a bouquet ~~for grandma.~~
I get them from the field. I rush with delight to give them to grandma.
I hand them to her but she can't reach. So I lay them on a stone.

Dandelions

I give her more yellow dandelions to make a bouquet for grandma,
I get them from the field. I rush with delight to give them to her.
I hand them to her but she can't reach. So I lay them on a stone.

On my second round of feedback, I again start with praise:

- "I notice you're trying to set a specific scene."
- "I see you've worked hard to tell a powerful and emotional story."
- "I notice you've added a title and adjusted the pronouns. I appreciate how I know, as the reader, who the two characters are in the first line."

To improve the poem, I ask Allison to look at the form. Allison still needs each line to contain between fourteen and sixteen syllables.

- "Unfortunately, you have too many syllables in the first line. Do you have an idea of what you can do to modify your structure to fit the sijo form? What can I do to assist you?"
- "On the next edit, can you focus on making the punctuation intentional?"

Allison reads my comments and then works in class with a partner to update her poem. Her partner says, "There is a lot of emotion in this last line. I think that this is a great twist, and I think you do a great job with sparking emotion within your reader."

At the end of the class period, Allison submits an updated draft to me:

Dandelions

I gather yellow dandelions to make a bouquet.
I get them from the field. I rush with delight to give them to grandma.
I hand them to her but she can't reach, so I lay them on a stone.

I read the poem a couple of times to absorb the changes. I am pleased with Allison's ability to tell an emotional and specific story and to elevate her piece through revision and collaboration. I say, "I like the characters and setting. You've also used the correct form. I'm really pleased with this poem if you are."

Allison submits this poem to a national sijo competition and is awarded third place and $300.

She said, "I learned about how I can express my feelings of loss. I learned that losing someone isn't always about frustration and pain; it's also about acceptance. I recently lost a family member, and after writing this poem, it helped me manage my grief … My mom is one of my best friends and she means the world to me. I read her my sijo while I was writing it, and she loved it, especially since the poem was written about her mom."

Paul Dressel, author of *Grades: One More Tilt at the Windmill*, wrote, "[A grade is] an inadequate report of an inaccurate judgment by a biased and variable judge of the extent to which a student has attained an undefined level of mastery of an unknown proportion of an indefinite material."

Grades are terrible feedback, but teachers can provide students with responses that encourage revision and growth. Consider the format of your feedback. Be timely and positive. Use questions to help students make changes and also to see their role in creating success. Assistance, not demands, encourages students to tackle revision and helps them engage with their learning. Successful feedback will build partnerships as students give and receive advice, not criticism.

Students can provide themselves or classmates with feedback. Model feedback loops for students before asking them to provide feedback independently. Assist students in accepting the comments as neutral and not taking suggestions personally.

We know students can be successful, and we need them to believe it too. Students need structured time and space to make changes and improve. Allow them to learn from their mistakes and to use class time to engage in valuable feedback loops.

RE-EVALUATE AND MOVE FORWARD
Build Resilience

You don't have to see the whole staircase, just take the first step.
— MARTIN LUTHER KING JR., MINISTER AND ACTIVIST

THE PROBLEM: Students don't evaluate their progress

"**I** STAYED UP ALL night," a student boasts about their last-minute schoolwork—writing a fifteen-page paper the night before it's due or pulling an all-nighter to study for an exam. The student wears their suffering as a badge of honor. The problem is what the student is bragging about: poor time management, avoidance, procrastination, and sleep deprivation.

Consider what one teacher experienced in a theater program: some students, mostly young women, had taken dance classes and quickly mastered complicated footwork. But other students, mostly young men who had spent years on a football team rather than on a dance team, were unfamiliar with chassé or heel-toe-heel-toe or shuffle-ball-change. They didn't know dance terminology or how to memorize eight-beat patterns.

Early rehearsals in the program featured a visiting choreographer who moved quickly, teaching each number. Those with dance experience mastered sequence after sequence, while other students fell behind. Instead of asking for help, those students faked the moves or hid in the back rows. Over and over, they practiced incorrect moves because they didn't want to admit they were lost. Then, after the visiting choreographer left, the theater teacher had to coach the students to undo their incorrect steps.

IN YOUR CLASSROOM, INSPIRE STUDENTS TO BUILD CONSISTENT PROGRESS WITH SMALL STEPS.

While the choreographer was there, the students who fell behind didn't evaluate their progress or their crisscrossed, incorrect steps. Instead of assessing and establishing a plan for improvement, they tried to mimic the path of more advanced students. They chose to save face rather than admit they needed help, so they had no chance of approaching each number with a logical, phrase-by-phrase approach.

THE HACK: Re-evaluate and move forward

Even with all the right measures in place, students can get stuck, and a process only works if students recognize mistakes, plan for improvement, and then keep moving forward in a positive and fruitful direction.

When students re-evaluate and move forward, they:

- acquire techniques
- build tiny habits, day after day
- apply self-control
- make mistakes when the stakes are low
- incorporate a choice that allows for another choice
- realize that every choice has a consequence

- focus on the controllables

- gain confidence

Assessing the process helps students realize there is more than one right answer or path. They just need to try, see how it goes, evaluate, and then try again.

Students will want to give up when things aren't easy, but this is not what builds a successful process. Help students design strategies that allow habits to become second nature. Normalize trying again and help students build a daily practice of progress. How can you assist students in showing up and putting in the work, especially when experiencing setbacks?

Students will not be excited for class every day, but they can make progress and learn even when they don't want to. Help them understand that making consistent progress puts them in a position to reach their goals. And as they make progress, celebrate each stage.

In your classroom, inspire students to build consistent progress with small steps. Practicing habits that move them in the right direction can create drastic and lasting changes. The key is to keep re-evaluating to decide the next best move.

Here are a few examples of habits for students to practice each day:

- Begin on time.

- Ignore (or limit time on) social media.

- Set a goal each day.

- Verbalize (or record) what you will accomplish today.

- Maintain a consistent order of operations, no matter the subject area.

- Finish (even if it's not perfect) your daily goal.

- Document the day's work.

Habits are specific behaviors repeated so regularly that they become automatic. Students need an environment that makes their target habits easy. If they struggle to implement a behavior, notice why and then work to help them make progress. If a student can't move forward because the task feels overwhelming, break it up. Can't do an hour-long study session? Start with five minutes. Struggling to read thirty pages? Start with three. Small progress is still progress.

When students are stuck, help them discover innovative ways to approach a project. Consider working backward. Violin teachers advise students to learn the last page first. They know that in a long piece, students can get bogged down. They start at the beginning, lose steam halfway through, and never learn the end. Likewise, all teachers may encourage students to work backward. On standardized tests, suggest students look at the multiple-choice answers first. When students know the possible answers, they are able to read the problem or passage with a purpose.

If not working backward, consider how technology may help students re-evaluate and move forward. If a student repeats words in a paragraph, suggest they use the find or search feature on their documents. If students can't get their ideas onto paper, suggest voice-to-text. When students struggle to organize their thoughts, a graphic organizer could illuminate themes. When students struggle with tone, diction, or making eye contact during a presentation, record the practice and give the student time to review the footage. Students could also take ideas and choreograph a dance or create a comic strip. An electronic form could be used to collect feedback or data. A news clip or TED Talk could bring additional insight.

Help students navigate challenges with an acceptance and responsibility mindset by:

- asking questions

- identifying roadblocks

- exhausting options

- making plans for improvement

- following through

If students say they're not in a good mental space, be patient. Help them move forward and create a process that maintains their momentum. First, model a process for students. Then, help students create a process with you. Finally, encourage them to design their own environments that will move them forward. Students need the process modeled first and then scaffolded with you before they will be able to do this independently.

Once the student starts, momentum helps them continue. It allows them to make another choice and to practice. Students will see that once they put in five minutes of studying or three minutes of reading, it's easier to continue with a few more minutes of studying or reading. Help your students understand that progress is not linear, but the goal is to trend upward. See Image 7.1.

PROGRESS IS NOT LINEAR; THE GOAL IS TO TREND UPWARD.

Image 7.1

Valerie King's seven-year-old students plan, create, manage, produce, and host a live daily news show. She said, "It would rival any high school media production." The experience happens every morning at school long before the first bell rings.

In this project, learners:

- explore and reflect on their strengths

- do one task better each day

- grow in confidence

- persist

- consider new things

- lead peers

- choose roles

King said, "One day, one of my learners was having a really challenging morning as our anchor. The director was trying to encourage her, but she had not practiced the script, and she was struggling."

King watched as emotions took over—and the production was beginning in moments. King asked the anchor if she wanted to continue for the show. She intimated that if she did, she needed to dry her eyes, put a smile on, and "find the joy" (a common phrase King uses with her students).

When the anchor couldn't get it together, the student opted for a peer to take her place. The next day, the student sat down at the anchor table and showed a different disposition. King asked, "What happened between yesterday and today?"

"I didn't do what I was supposed to in order to be ready for the show yesterday. So, now I made sure I practiced. Before the show, I took a deep breath and knew I could do it."

King found this impressive: her seven-year-old student moved through the process with very little teacher facilitation. King said, "For the youngest learners, the expectations need to be high and the context for learning safe to think and continually re-evaluate in order to move forward."

No matter the subject area or grade level, our job is to help students re-evaluate and move forward. As students work, build in time to truly experience reading or drawing or mathematics. As students move through the class period, ask them to describe how they feel, what they see, and to acknowledge what is going well and what isn't—without judgment. Encourage students to be resilient and celebrate mistakes because they make us stronger, smarter, and better able to see what is important.

To encourage choir students to produce a successful rehearsal, teachers establish a consistent routine that students can use when practicing at home. They remove backpacks and cellphones from the rehearsal area, throw out gum, review the order of rehearsal, and begin warm-ups from the piano. In a physical education class, students re-evaluate and move forward through each unit. During the swim unit, the teacher prompts students to identify what they can control. This shows students that focusing on the little things leads to the greatest of things. The following is an example process for swim class that students could evaluate:

- Show up to class on time with a swimsuit, cap, and towel.

- Bring water bottles to practice hydration.

- Before getting in the pool, stretch on the deck and warm up the body and mind.

- Discuss mentality and practice visualization.

- Study meet rules and disqualifications.

- Hone skills like flip turns and strokes.

- Write in journals to record workouts and how they went.

At the end of the unit, swimmers implement the system used during class at a meet. They write events, heats, and lanes on their arms. Each athlete has multiple events, and instead of relying on others (teammates, coaches, or parents) to tell them when and where to be for each race, this process helps each athlete manage the meet themselves.

Your own constant evaluation of student progress is not essential. Instead, allow students to take a task in front of them and put it behind them. This helps them feel pride and accomplishment, which builds satisfaction and momentum. It also allows students to see they are the owners and designers of their process and progress.

As students move through the process, they can self-evaluate and use their feedback along with input from you and their classmates. What is not necessary? What pieces can be eliminated? Their process will change, and that is okay; they just need to keep evaluating and adjusting.

In the classroom and in life, habits are momentum. They keep each person going, even when they tire, falter, or lack motivation or willpower. Throughout the process, students can expect discomfort, but they possess skills to overcome challenges: curiosity, compassion, resolve, and drive. They can evaluate, make changes, and try again.

With this type of evaluation, students may also notice how their process differs from others. Assist students in identifying the differences in processes in order to capitalize on them. How can they turn their uniqueness into an advantage? (For more about positive comparisons, see Hack 4: Produce Positive Competition.) Anyone who reaches the rarefied air of extraordinary accomplishment has put in time and effort. They have done the work, listened, and learned from those who came before them. They have not changed who they are, but they have capitalized on it. Process-based assessment allows students to identify their own strengths. A fruitful and successful process is not driven by grades; however, assessment helps students progress.

In the words of my students:

> "The fact that every assignment is either a one or zero really made me not procrastinate and complete my assignments on time for this class. This policy not only made me improve my writing, but also helped get rid of my bad school habits."

> "The biggest difference between this class and others is that it had no quizzes and tests. We did not learn anything that needed to be memorized and tested. Instead, we practiced

applying concepts every day in our writing. The open-ended style hits home and I like how it does not push us into boxes. From the grading system, I learned the importance of making the most of a stretch of time, since I could not drag my feet when working during class and then make it up later."

"This was very different from any other class I have taken. The rules were not different, but what was expected was different. In this class I was expected to find success in some writing forms and terribly fail in others. Making mistakes in this class is what led to breakthroughs in my writing because I felt comfortable trying something new without the fear of a bad grade. The point system, with no late work, fits this class perfectly because I was encouraged to try new things and be creative and I was given plenty of opportunities to work in class."

"I really enjoyed the point and no late work system in this class. It was a relief not being overwhelmed with homework from this class as well. I thought that the point system was beneficial because I was able to express my thoughts and not worry about making sure I was writing A-quality work. Instead, I was able to enjoy writing and not worry about what my grade was going to be. I also think that this took a lot of pressure and stress off which was very nice. I also really liked that I was never rushed into writing my pieces. I was able to have multiple days to work on and draft my pieces."

● ● ●

I was looking for writers' markets to motivate my students when I came upon the Sejong Cultural Society's sijo competition, offered in collaboration with the Korea Institute at Harvard University.

I didn't know what sijo was, so I read example poems, devoured articles, and watched lectures. I learned sijo is a beautiful poetic form similar to haiku.

The first year I shared the national poetry contest with my

students, two of them were selected as winners. I was energized to continue sharing the competition with my students. But then, for two years, I didn't have any winners. I didn't focus on my poor outcome. Instead, I dove deeper into my learning; I analyzed more winning poems, hunting for themes. I asked questions of poetry experts and attended conferences. I wanted to know more about the sijo form. I wanted to help my students create more beautiful or more powerful poems.

Over the next two years, I had a bit of success (two of my students received honorable mentions), and then the Sejong Cultural Society reached out to me. Dr. Lucy Park, the executive director, said she was impressed with my students' entries—so much so, she wanted to record my lessons for other teachers to study.

I barely felt like I knew what I was doing, but I agreed. If Dr. Park recognized my students' entries, I must be doing something right.

Then, in 2016, I had a first-place winner and an honorable mention. Between 2017 and 2020, fourteen of my students were recognized. The success helped me gain confidence, and I wanted to help other teachers inspire their students through poetry. I wrote articles for *Edutopia* and *Teachers & Writers Magazine*. I presented about sijo at conferences. I kept learning and growing my knowledge, not only of sijo but also of East Asia and poetry.

In 2020, I sat in a professional development class at UW-Madison. I was there to study the Korean War. When I mentioned my love for sijo to the professor, he asked how we could use the poetry form to get Wisconsinites engaged with East Asian culture. I suggested he connect with Dr. Park, and soon, they offered a sijo competition just for Wisconsin residents.

When I stumbled upon the Sejong Cultural Society's competition over a decade ago, I could not have known where my voyage would lead. I could have abandoned the project when my students' work wasn't recognized. Instead, I evaluated and improved my process. I kept learning, and I put in the work.

Today, I am one of a handful of sijo experts in the United States. I co-edited *SIJO Korea's Poetry Form*, a primer featuring the work of Dr. Park, Newbery Medal winner Linda Sue Park, Harvard Professor Dr. David McCann, and Brigham Young University Professor Emeritus Dr. Mark Peterson, among others. I am eager to see where the next step of the process leads.

UNTITLED BY ELIZABETH JORGENSEN

I called on the smallest student, the one hiding in the back.
"I have nothing," she said. She cradled her head in her hands.
I didn't respond; instead, waited; willed her to fill the silence.

Image 7.2: The 2021 Wisconsin Sijo Competition runner-up poem.

WHAT YOU CAN DO TOMORROW

There is no black or white, no right or wrong. There is only what works. Conversations with your students can assist them in realizing they can't control what happens to them, but they can re-evaluate and move forward; they can control how they respond and react to road-blocks or challenges.

- **Troubleshoot scenarios with students.** Present your students with a fictitious scenario and ask them to target specific habits or behaviors that would allow the student in the example to move forward. Provide in-class time for the students to share their answers; facilitate conversations and ask students to brainstorm additional useful habits and behaviors.
  - ▸ *Example scenario:* A student aims to apply for ten internships before the end of the semester.

> ▸ *Roadblocks:* On weekdays, the student cares for his two younger siblings. On weekends, he works eight hours at a restaurant. He also volunteers at an animal shelter and plays intramural badminton. He received a C in his last English class and doesn't view himself as a competent communicator.

- **Share "failure" role models.** In bookstores and libraries, shelves are filled with how-to books. People naturally want to get better, and that's why these books exist. Kids want to improve too. Ask students who they admire, and search for books and quotes by those writers. If students are interested in sports, remind them about the famous Michael Jordan quote: "I've missed more than nine thousand shots in my career. I've lost almost three hundred games. Twenty-six times, I've been trusted to take the game-winning shot and missed. I've failed over and over and over again in my life. And that is why I succeed." Jordan failed repeatedly, and that's how he found success. Author J. K. Rowling submitted her manuscript over and over and was rejected, yet her Harry Potter series became a bestseller. President Joe Biden stuttered, but he learned how to keep moving and spoke to millions on television as the president. King George VI of England also overcame a stutter as a public figure.

  Even products can serve as role models. For example, WD-40 and Formula 409 have names that represent the number of attempts before the successful formula.

- **Share about yourself.** Students enjoy hearing about you. Discuss with students how life is a series of unknowns. When you were a teenager, did you know what you wanted to do with your life? The city you wanted to live in? Where you wanted to work? From which job you wanted to retire? How did you keep moving forward through the unknowns? How did you build and maintain momentum? What processes and habits helped you along? How did your mindset help you? How did you follow what you were interested in to get where you are? Foster community and connection through dialogue.

- **Teach students about metacognition.** Ask students to reflect on a habit they've developed and successfully implemented. How did their process maintain their momentum? How could this process aid other performances? Students can also identify a behavior that's not sticking. How can they work through their feelings and thoughts to change their actions? What skills have they already developed that they can apply to challenging situations?

A BLUEPRINT FOR FULL IMPLEMENTATION

When students experience challenges, help them to re-evaluate and move forward. Lasting change is not about motivation or self-control. It's about strategic habits executed day after day; it's about getting students to start in order to maintain their momentum.

Step 1: See the big picture and remain compassionate and pleasant.

To get students to move forward, rely on relationships. Appreciating and valuing each student's process requires you to know and meet students where they are. Psychology, mental health, and the student/ teacher relationship impact performance. Encourage students to share what's going on in their lives. Only when we know what's going on can we confidently assist students in re-evaluating and moving forward.

On assignments, consider asking students to leave an "assignment note." Students can use this space to share how they're feeling about what they did or, conversely, what prevented their progress. The assignment note may include an evaluation and a plan for forward movement during the subsequent classes.

Step 2: Eliminate interference.

Brains are constantly looking for more entertainment or stimulation. Create an environment that minimizes distraction. Ask students to place cellphones in shoe holders during class (see Image 7.3). When possible, ask them to put away computers or tablets and use paper and pencil. Give students the best shot at focusing on and enjoying the classroom experience.

Image 7.3

Step 3: Identify process-friendly spaces.

Will students write while lounging in their favorite bean bag? In their bed? On the bleachers after practice? At the library during study hall? Will they use cursive or lined paper or a keyboard?

Ask students to share what time they'll start, where they'll sit, and which device they'll use. The more specific, the more likely the student will be to follow the plan. This will help students move forward even when they don't want to or even when tasks are difficult. It will also help students adjust if the process isn't successful.

Step 4: Diagnose productivity.

Have students name behaviors that need modification. If seating was uncomfortable, what could they try next? If they were distracted by the dog, what other locations might work? If writing didn't work, could they draw a picture or compose an outline or ask a friend or family member to collaborate?

Additionally, ask students to identify behaviors that were successful. What worked? How can the student maintain their momentum?

Assessing a student's process holds them accountable for making the most of their work time. As students produce, they'll gather data and realize what is working and what isn't. The more students know, the better decisions they can make. Encourage them to make a decision that lets them make another, and take it one decision at a time. See Image 7.4 for an example of student-set daily goals.

STUDENT-SET DAILY GOALS:

Ask questions
Learn more
Explore a passion
Develop hypotheses
Test theories
Identify obstacles
Come up with more questions
Make progress
Solicit feedback

Image 7.4

Step 5: Keep moving every day.

Incremental gains build transformative changes, but the hardest part is starting. Use cues to signal behaviors. You may want to use a bell at the beginning of the hour and start with the same warmup or your class mantra. Routines keep behaviors going.

To increase production, provide students with the opportunity to practice and to use class time to choose what is important; remind students that each choice reflects what they value. To keep the momentum going outside of class, ask students to record their progress. For example:

- An acting or music class implements rehearsal charts where kids record their home practice and have a parent or guardian sign.

- Summer library programs instill daily reading habits when they offer awards and rewards for books read.

- Comedian Jerry Seinfeld writes a joke every day. He uses a wall calendar that displays the whole year. After writing his daily joke, he checks off the date. Seinfeld says, "Just keep at it, and the chain will grow longer every day. You'll like seeing that chain, especially when you get a few weeks under your belt. Your only job next is to not break the chain." Jerry's goal is not to write a quality or funny joke but to write a joke and move forward.

Step 6: Create a safe space.

When a student puts in the time and effort to attempt a task and, despite their engagement, the result isn't successful, celebrate what they achieved. Call it a win. They showed up, put in the work, and asked questions. They exhibited grit and model-worthy decisions. They had the guts to attempt a task they were uncertain about. They were brave.

A safe space is not about the teacher solving problems but about students figuring out what works best for their process. If a student stresses about a past mistake, they go through the negative experience twice. We don't want students to dwell on mistakes. Instead, we want to help students accept the setback as neutral data and focus on what they need to change to go forward.

The most challenging days can be the most important. The student did something, they kept the momentum moving, and they looked at the setback as an opportunity to improve. When a mistake happens, encourage students to ask themselves: "How can I make a little more progress? How can I get a little better?"

Lead by example and share with your students a time when you failed and how failing led to success. How did you stay positive and move forward? Explain your resilience. Did you rely on your colleagues or friends and family? Did you practice mindfulness or yoga? Did you stay away from social media or negative influences?

Reframing is a habit that can direct students to a more successful process, to focus on the goal, and to not give up. Ask students about a time when they failed or to explain an issue that challenges them and why. Encourage students to discuss what helps them move forward and to see setbacks as pathways to assess, evaluate, and try again.

OVERCOMING PUSHBACK

Students spend too much time thinking. We want them to do. We know our students will fail at times, and they should. The key is to help students develop a growth mindset that helps them re-evaluate and move forward.

The habits aren't sticking. The process of practice is not linear, and sometimes, when students realize this, they want to give up. When habits don't stick, students feel stuck. You are a supportive and secure presence, and this breeds confidence, allowing students to make progress and try again. Students often think the tasks in front of them are impossible and that even if they tried, they'd fail. When students get overwhelmed, it's often because they don't know where to start or what is most important. To help support students, ask them to try one of the following three practices.

- *Make a list.* Just writing down tasks helps students realize there isn't as much to do as they originally thought, and they can control their progress. Here's one way my students listed their steps so they could organize their thoughts and take control of their processes:
  1) Write down everything that needs to happen.
  2) Organize the list by what needs to happen immediately, what can wait, and what can be delegated.
  3) Take the list one item at a time. 4) Share feelings or progress at the end of the class period.

- *Find role models who are successful and inspiring.* Consider sports figures like Kobe Bryant or Vince Lombardi. My students enjoy reading Bryant's poem *Dear Basketball.* While some students comment on how they didn't know Bryant was a poet, other students reference his book *The Mamba Mentality: How I Play.* One Wisconsin teacher instituted "Lombardi time" in her classes and with her extracurricular groups. She told her students the story of Lombardi and how he fired a player for being on time. She explained that to Lombardi, if a player was on time, they were late. He expected his players to always arrive fifteen minutes early. Her students still mention this tradition on social media.

- *Practice visualization or mindfulness strategies.* Mindfulness helps build students' resolve. It also reminds them of what they can control: their actions or habits. You and your students may want to try these modifications of common therapeutic techniques for centering or calming:

  ‣ Take a three-second breath every time you sit at your desk. (Students encounter a desk multiple times each day. The three-second breath can be a reminder to remain present.)

  ‣ Ask students to describe five things they can see, four things they can feel, three things they can hear, two things they can smell, and one thing they can taste.

  ‣ Ask students to describe five things that start with the same letter. Five things that are the same color. Five things that are smooth. Five things that are square. Five things that are dull.

  ‣ Use square breathing (also called box breathing). As students trace a box, they breathe in for four counts and out for four counts, all the way around the box. Students should relax their jaw and forehead and use deep breaths, in through the nose and out the mouth. A similar strategy is to trace the hand while breathing in and out.

- *Complete a task with the non-dominant hand.*

  ‣ Sometimes, students try to accomplish too much too soon. Help them learn to break a project down into manageable steps. When piano students are at an impasse, the teacher often recommends playing only the left hand. Then, play only the right hand.

The students are frustrated. Learning should not feel hard; it should feel sustainable. Every project, decision, problem, and challenge is different, so different solutions will work at different times. When students get frustrated, help them take one thought, one task, and one day at a time. Help students:

- gain confidence in their judgment

- surround themselves with trusted sources

- build in time for collaboration

- recognize where progress comes from: showing up and doing

- take control of moving forward and managing their momentum

Students refuse to try. Beginnings are difficult, and teachers need to respond with support, approval, and encouragement. Remind students that although it's easy to practice when they're at their best or tasks are easy, it's challenging to show up when they feel like nothing works. Honor how your students feel and recognize that everyone can do the former, but the latter has the larger impact.

What barriers can students construct to put between themselves and the habits that don't work? For example, if they keep checking social media instead of doing their schoolwork, what process adjustments could they make?

There's not enough time to have these conversations and construct these processes with each student. Consider pairing students who either have similar or dissimilar struggles. If one student always finishes early, can you pair him with someone who struggles to start? What can they learn from each other's processes? Or if several students struggle with a concept, can they brainstorm road-blocks and test solutions together? Evaluation can be done in pairs, small groups, or as a whole class. Conversations do not need to be teacher-driven.

THE HACK IN ACTION

In her second grade class, Valerie King's seven-year-old students crafted a Civil War replica steam locomotive out of cafeteria milk cartons. It was a monumental task, and while the design process was noteworthy, more important were the evolving habits of thinking.

One day, a group of learners built a car to attach to the engine. They had graphed and calculated dimensions, but King saw an error. One side of the rectangular building looked to be five milk cartons smaller than the other side. It would have been easy for King to interrupt the process and fix her students' thinking. But she didn't. Instead, she observed the group counting and recounting and heard one learner say, "I think something might be off. Let me count again."

Even though the recount was still incorrect, King continued to let them build. Her students used low-temperature hot-glue guns, and while her grown-up experience knew they were going to be too far ahead to make this an easy fix, she continued to let them work.

After the entire frame was built, the group realized their error.

King says, "I will never forget the look on Tyler's face, as he was the first to realize. He said, 'Uhm. I think one of the sides is wrong.' As he stood the rectangular frame base on its end and watched it wobble, he said, 'What can we do?'"

King shrugged her shoulders and said, "I believe your group can solve this problem together."

RIGIDITY DOESN'T LEAD TO LONG-TERM PROGRESS. INSTEAD, EMPOWER STUDENTS AND EQUIP THEM WITH THE SKILLS TO ADAPT.

And they did. They counted how many milk cartons needed to be removed and then reattached what was left, and it worked out.

During the reflection, King asked, "What new thing did you learn today?"

While most groups focused on "How to listen to new ideas" or "How to scale a drawing," Tyler's group said, "We learned that before we finish something, we need to stop and check and see if we are on the right track."

An intentional move from King allowed her learners to fail, think, evaluate, and realize the importance of checking in on their process.

One of Thomas Edison's famous quotes sums up this Hack nicely. He said, "I have not failed. I've just found ten thousand ways that won't work."

Students need reminders that progress does not always trend upward, and progress does not come in one way; there will be days when things don't work out. That is okay; the classroom is a safe space to try, fail, learn, and move forward. Focus on each individual student's improvement and not their results. Help students push themselves, stay consistent, be patient, and never give up.

Today, progress could mean one more math problem successfully solved or one more vocabulary word correctly spelled. Tomorrow, it could mean inventing a machine or writing a book. Recognize your students' progress as it happens, however it happens, and know that tomorrow's progress will look different.

Rigidity doesn't lead to long-term progress. Instead, empower students and equip them with the skills to adapt. Help students care about their work. Build trust in the process, and engineer mechanisms that make the process work. Allow for student interest. Celebrate successes and challenges, share them, and then, go on improving.

In the classroom, the only thing that matters is what students do right now. It's not about being perfect but about being good enough and then doing it again tomorrow. Like author James Clear suggests, "Reading 20 pages per day is 30 books per year. Saving $10 per day is $3,650 a year. Running 1 mile per day is 365 miles per year. Becoming 1 percent better per day is 37 percent better per year. Small habits are underestimated."

FIND A PURPOSE
Create Authentic Learning Opportunities

Tell me and I forget. Teach me and I remember. Involve me and I learn.
— Benjamin Franklin, founding father of the United States

THE PROBLEM: Students don't care about their work

MANY STUDENTS SEE assignments as busywork—boxes to check or hoops to jump through. When students think this way, they aren't invested in their work. They don't see the purpose of it, so they don't attempt the task. This disengagement manifests behavior issues. Paper airplanes fly. Students doodle on the desk. They tap the classmate in front of them. They try to get reactions from peers with jokes or distractions. They look for entertainment on social media or in streaming services.

Teachers then spend instructional time redirecting students to "pull out your packet" or "take your notes" or "sit down." But for what? To get students to complete an assignment for a grade?

Without an authentic purpose for the work, students lack

motivation or resolve. Although grades may be enough motivation for some, even the most dedicated students struggle with engagement the days before a holiday break. This is why teachers put on movies or plan parties.

THE HACK: Find a purpose

Authentic purposes connect students to opportunities outside your classroom, engage them in the learning, and allow you to work alongside your students to reach a shared goal. When young people engage with their community, they find relevance in their work and the motivation to improve their processes.

As a teacher and author, I share my writing process with students. When my co-written memoir, *Go, Gwen, Go: A Family's Journey to Olympic Gold*, was published (see Image 8.1), I presented to classes at my school and in my community. After my presentation, students responded on the memoir's theme of perseverance, the writing and publishing process, and about what they learned that applies to their lives.

Student reactions to the theme of perseverance:

"While I might not choose to write a book, you encouraged me to have strong dedication and passion for the goals I love."

"I took it to heart when you said if someone says you're good at something, then listen to them and do it!"

"I was encouraged to get involved more with what I love. You showed me how I can take risks."

Student reactions to writing and publishing:

"I learned that writing is a very long, continuous process and rejection is necessary. I also learned that feedback is very important from numerous people to make you a better writer."

"I learned that you don't have to write from the perspective of the main character to get the story across."

"I learned that you can't give up right away because you are going to get turned down by many people and publishers but you have to just keep making revisions and believing that your work deserves to be published."

"The big thing I learned is that writing takes time. If it took almost seven years to complete your book, that means I should be spending more time on my essays."

"I truly appreciated learning about what goes on behind the scenes to publish a book. I learned about how long it took to write and publish and the amount of people actually involved in editing. I learned that you may go through hundreds of rough drafts and ideas before you even show anyone and then after you get feedback, there's still more to do."

Student reactions to life applications:

"You taught us that it is okay to fail but it is important to learn from it and continue what you started."

"My life can be completely changed on a certain day of the week because of the opportunities and the people I meet."

"What I learned is that hard work is a good thing. If you put in hard work, a positive outcome is more of a possibility."

Inviting professionals into your classroom makes learning personal and purposeful—and it may even inspire students to see what is possible for them both inside and outside the classroom. Consider contacting authors your students read. Many of them offer no-fee presentations to schools.

Image 8.1

After surveying classes in my school, I found these examples of authentic learning. Look for similar examples and opportunities in your school.

- Students in an art class submit portfolios to art competitions, display art in the school commons, and participate in a community art show.

- Students in a marketing class host a Marketing Night at a school basketball game. Students coordinate the event, including giveaways, mascot performances, and halftime entertainment. Money raised is donated to a charitable cause.

- Students in Distributive Education Clubs of America (DECA) send handmade cards and handwritten letters to senior citizens in nursing homes.

- Students in a technical education class sell lawn decorations and furniture to the community and host manufacturing workshops for teachers, parents, and community members.

- Students in a band class perform in concerts and at music festivals.

- Students in an acting class put on a showcase for friends, family, and the community.

- Students in an English class publish a class newsletter, write letters to veterans going on an Honor Flight, keep a blog, and enter essays into scholarship competitions.

- Students in a physical education class participate in a high ropes course and mentor a youth team.

- Students in a science class tour a laboratory and visit a museum for hands-on experiences.

- Students in an engineering and mechanics class build ball launchers based on equations.

- Students in a landscape ecology class plant and manage seeds for an annual sale. The sale includes vegetables, herbs, and perennial wildflowers. Customers include faculty, staff, relatives, students, parents, and community members.

- Students in a food and consumer education class operate and manage food trucks and sell snacks in the cafeteria.

- Students in a high school class partner with students in an elementary class for a collaborative project.

- Students complete job shadows and internships.

- Students write letters to change-makers, to people with purchasing power, and to government officials.

- Students do hands-on volunteer work.

- Students hear from guest speakers.

● ● ●

Mary Witte teaches middle school math, and she created Project Reality, an economic-based financial literacy program that engages students in real-life experiences. Throughout Project Reality, her students tour businesses and hear from guest speakers. Witte said, "I want students to realize that college isn't the only path."

At Empire Level, a factory in the students' hometown, her students learn from employees. Witte said, "Students begin to actively prepare for their futures."

Witte realizes that many of our nation's students leave college with mounds of accumulating debt. Witte uses Project Reality to help students prepare for freedom, happiness, and the financial choices they will make. Witte's students choose a job and then complete balance sheets, purchase a home and car, and plan for vacations. In addition to studying the stock market and compounding interest, her students learn responsibility, professionalism, and how choices today affect the future.

She said, "I see a love of learning when I bring real-life situations to the classroom." Bankers speak to students during guest lectures, and they either approve or deny car loans. "Students learn how much that truck actually costs and how much they have to make to afford it," she said.

To prepare for guest speakers and tours, students write resumes, complete job applications, and participate in mock interviews.

Witte also shares scholarship opportunities. "Although my students are in seventh grade, they learn about the scholarships they can earn as early as eighth grade. This helps students realize they can start now taking control of their finances. Students get so excited when they come back and tell me they earned their first scholarship," she said.

In the gradebook, Witte's students receive a pass or fail during each grading period in the unit. If a student's balance sheet is above $0, they pass. "Students know if they are going to pass or not and can earn additional money if they are at risk," she said. "They're invested, so I just am there to answer questions and make sure they stay on track. Student engagement increases because they have the power. I enjoy watching them learn not only about financial literacy but also about integrity, respect, and teamwork."

WHEN STUDENTS INTERACT OUTSIDE THE CLASSROOM, THEY LEARN THAT IF THEY'RE VULNERABLE, TAKE A RISK, AND PUT IN THE DAILY EFFORT, THEY CAN SEE AMAZING RESULTS.

Authentic purposes like Project Reality help students focus on the experience and process, not the grade. Authentic learning includes so many benefits. Here are a few of the benefits, according to students:

- Student Jamal said his favorite part of the engineering and mechanics class was the ball launcher. He said, "Before this class, I didn't like the engineering process because I thought documenting everything was a waste of time. But now, I realize how important it is."

- Student Mark said, "Engineering gives that same satisfying result when I spend weeks working on a project and watching it run smooth as butter. I've taken Introduction to Engineering, Engineering Mechanics, and currently, in Woodshop I, I'm yet to dislike one of them. I love working hard for weeks and sometimes months on a project and watching it run perfectly on the due date. The entire engineering process I find fascinating. From programming and modeling on the computer then off to the machines to begin the building process, to the testing phase, and finally, the time to present my work—it's all amazing."

- Student Nicki submitted essays into writing competitions. The Milwaukee Society of Plastics Engineers selected her essay for first place, and she was published in *Teaching Today Wisconsin*. Nicki's confidence catapulted, and she began to view herself as a competent and skilled writer. Nicki said, "I am excited to keep on doing more writing competitions and to keep working to get my writing published. ... I have really grown a lot as a writer so far this year ... writing has really changed how I look at the world."

When students interact inside or outside the classroom, they learn that if they're vulnerable, take a risk, and put in the daily effort, they can see amazing results. And even if they don't receive the results they aimed for, they feel satisfied. They gave it their all, they couldn't have done anything more, and they found meaning in their work beyond a grade.

WHAT YOU CAN DO TOMORROW

Your community is your ally and asset. Reach out to professionals at local nonprofit organizations, museums, universities, or libraries to build inventive, student-centered experiences. Community members can connect you with authentic opportunities for students or help you find volunteers who can present to your class or your school. Think creatively about who might be able to assist you in coordinating authentic opportunities for your students.

- **Connect with nursing homes.** Many nursing homes welcome interactions with young people. Most are accustomed to holiday caroling, but students could also read to residents, perform skits, or create puzzles or games. History and journalism students could interview residents and write essays about residents' lives. English students could organize a student/resident book club or pen pal exchange.

- **Solicit community members.** Send an email to your students' guardians, soliciting their support or input. Mention authentic learning opportunities at Open House or parent/teacher conferences. A guardian might welcome your class to shadow a manufacturing facility, coordinate a trip to a field research center, or present to your classes.

  My students read a column from our hometown newspaper: *Snapshots* by Crocker Stephenson. Stephenson interviews community members and tells compelling stories. My students enjoyed his column so much that I contacted him, and

Stephenson offered to present on his writing process as well as the journalism profession. All students in the school were invited to the event in the school auditorium.

The Wisconsin poet laureate presented to my classes, and students heard firsthand about careers tied to writing and the arts. After her presentation, students said they felt inspired and that they enjoyed learning and practicing new literary techniques.

- **Talk with colleagues.** How do they make learning authentic? How do they assess and coordinate those experiences? How can you partner with them in already-established activities?

  Jake Polancich, a high school band director, programmed *Variations on a Korean Folk Song* (which are based on *Arirang*, the unofficial anthem of Korea). In teaching his students about Korean culture, he asked me to speak to his band members about Korean poetry. After my presentation, each of his students wrote a poem in a Korean form of poetry. Several were included in the concert program. Polancich also encouraged his students to submit poems to publications or competitions.

- **Consider students' ideas.** Students are innovative and creative; allow them to propose ideas for a collaboration. Students in the National Honor Society may be looking to earn volunteer hours, and those in other organizations, like Key Club or Optimist International, might be willing to partner with your students or volunteer in your classroom.

A BLUEPRINT FOR FULL IMPLEMENTATION

When students work for an authentic purpose, they are more motivated and invested in their process. They increase their effort because they know someone other than their teacher will see their performance or work. It can be time-consuming to coordinate learning tied to authentic experiences, but the benefits make your investment worth it.

Step 1: Find a specific purpose for student work.

Discover opportunities in the local media or on social media. Gather inspiration from your colleagues or your students' families. Conferences and teacher publications are also good places to explore.

Step 2: Engineer your lessons, working backward.

Use the requirements of the authentic purpose as your guide. What do you want students to accomplish or gain from the experience? What do students need to master before participating?

When students participate in the Wisconsin Solo & Ensemble Festival, directors consider the following:

- When is the music festival?
- What are the entry requirements?
- Who will choose the literature?
- Who will choose the groups?
- When do entries need to be submitted?
- Who will enter them?
- How is the fee paid?
- How will students coordinate with accompanists?
- How will students get to the venue?

- Is there a dress code?

- Is there a school code of conduct for events off-campus?

- How will parents be informed?

- What if someone falls ill?

- How will students know when they are ready to compete?

- What's the incentive or reward for participation—grade, point, or advance to the next level?

Step 3: Plan authentic learning experiences in advance.

Speak with your administrators and ask for assistance in managing and implementing logistics. Consider transportation and parental approval. If you plan to bring in members of the community, are background checks necessary?

If live experiences are not an option, consider virtual experiences.

- Students can take virtual tours of the Museum of the World, the Smithsonian, The Dali Museum, Museo Nacional del Prado, Paris Musées, Great Wall of China, Buckingham Palace, Machu Picchu, or the Taj Mahal.

- You can arrange virtual presentations with authors, alumni, and professors. Some organizations, like the Pulitzer Center, offer live virtual workshops and guest speakers. Local journalists or poet laureates may also offer complimentary presentations.

Step 4: Introduce the opportunity to students and allow them time to prepare.

Practice and revision should happen frequently before students engage with the authentic learning opportunity. Prepare students so they go into the experience with confidence. Help them understand their role and set clear expectations. Do students need to read some of the journalist's work before he presents? Do they need to prepare questions? Build skills and practice habits students need to be successful. Students may need instruction or lessons on email etiquette, business attire, or workplace norms. Help them to anticipate challenges and plan for setbacks. Ask them to brainstorm and discuss accommodations. What should they do if the Wi-Fi goes out? What should they do if they are ill? What if they forget the lyrics mid-song?

Step 5: Participate in the experience.

Students will likely feel nervous or cautious. Remind them of their hard work, of how they prepared, and of how they built skills and practiced habits. Repeat the class mantra. Remind students of their vision board. As students participate, enjoy the experience but also notice what you can do to make the experience better next time.

Step 6: Share successes.

Highlight the results of the authentic learning opportunity within your school and community. Suggest that your school's administration post photographs or press releases to their social media pages or on the school website. Contact your local newspapers for a feature.

Step 7: Celebrate all students.

When the authentic learning opportunity is over, allow time to honor the work and progress. Send congratulatory emails to the students and copy their guardians on the messages. Consider displaying work, posting photographs, creating videos, and sending thank-you notes. Even if students aren't pleased with their results, all students should be celebrated. They put themselves out there, took a risk, and shared their skills and talents with the community.

OVERCOMING PUSHBACK

Authentic learning opportunities are possibilities. They do not guarantee success, and often, they come with more work and challenges than you anticipated. However, the rewards are worth the risks when students find a purpose for their work and care about their effort.

Parents and guardians want to protect their students' privacy. Connecting students with the community might include publicity and media photos or sharing email addresses, student names, and phone numbers. Reference your school's student directory; note which guardians requested their student's data be withheld. Pay attention to what data was restricted (phone number, email, likeness, or name) and respect these wishes. If there's any question about participating, call the guardian and explain the event or opportunity. If guardians request their student not participate, students can still work alongside their classmates, completing the same preparatory work. In these rare cases, the only part of the unit the student needs to miss is submitting or sharing with an audience outside the classroom. Students may also be able to participate anonymously.

SHARING A TIME WHEN YOU WERE VULNERABLE WILL REMIND STUDENTS THEY'RE NOT ALONE.

Students are uncomfortable sharing with outside sources. Explain to your students the benefits of the authentic learning opportunity. They may not understand why they would want to be published or win an award or participate in the competition or hear from a professional. They might also be scared, especially if they've never done this before. Walk through the entire project with them and invite others to join the process: parents, grandparents, siblings, and friends. Make the activity a community affair. Participate alongside your students when possible. When students see they're not alone, they're more likely to feel comfortable engaging with the world.

What about the students who don't perform well? When students participate in authentic learning opportunities, they can be scared and reticent. What if they're rejected? What if they don't get the result they seek? What if things go awry? Sharing a time when you were vulnerable will remind students they're not alone. This is also a great way for students to see that teachers are learners too. What did you learn when you submitted a conference proposal that was rejected? What happened when you kept trying, were accepted, and gave your first presentation? What did you learn? What perspectives did you gain? What connections did you make?

When participating in authentic learning opportunities, the goal is not to win or to be the best but to increase engagement and appreciate growth. Help your students focus on gaining excitement, learning from the experience, making connections, and enjoying the process of sharing and performing. The feedback students receive from the experience (both positive and constructive) helps them understand their performance's effectiveness. It also reveals the subjective and complex nature of competition and judgment.

But it's so much work. Participating in authentic learning opportunities takes attention to detail, precise planning, and paperwork. It is exponentially more work than keeping student work inside your classroom. But it's worth it when you consider student gains. And, once you've coordinated these experiences a few times, they become easier. You've established connections, you've learned from mistakes, and you've streamlined the process.

THE HACK IN ACTION

I met Kate Van Haren while participating in an online Korean War Teaching Initiative offered by the University of Wisconsin-Madison. We saw an opportunity for our students to benefit from collaboration across grade levels and across the state.

Because our students are in upper elementary and high school and live over three hours away from each other, we collaborated electronically to create a book written, edited, illustrated, and read by our elementary and high school students. The collaboration provided a genuine purpose: students practiced mentorship and created pieces for an audience.

Elementary school students said:

> "It was so cool to work with older kids. I can't wait to improve my writing so I can write like them. I feel inspired!"

> "I like that I got to pick a topic that I wanted to write about."

> "It's been kind of lonely because we can't work in groups this year [because of the pandemic]. I like being able to work with different people even if it was through the computer."

High school students said:

> "Reading the younger students' poems was a cool experience! I got to exercise giving feedback. I thought it was cool to read everything out loud because it's a different experience than just reading it on a screen."

> "I thought the collaboration was very beneficial for everyone. It helped the elementary students with quality feedback and it also helped the high school students by making them understand poetry enough to teach it."

> "A lot of the younger students had really good ideas and it was so cool to see their progress. I learned to be patient and understanding during this collaboration."

> "Something I got out of this was seeing a poem from a younger perspective ... It was nice to be able to work with a much different age group. It definitely gave me a reflection of how writing styles change as we age. It's interesting to see how these kids interpret things now."

Students were excited to collaborate with their cross-grade partners, apply updates, and continue the writing process. Van Haren said her students were more engaged than they would have been with just teacher comments.

Each page in the book featured one elementary school student (their name, topic, poem, illustration, and high school partners) and a link to a recording of them reading their poem.

When the book was complete, it was presented to the school board, and an e-book link was posted on our schools' social media pages. Community members were encouraged to provide feedback through Flipgrid.

Bryan, a senior, said:

> "I think I really found a hidden poet within myself. One thing I learned about myself is that I can be a good writer, I just need to practice."

Landyn, an elementary school student, summed up the opinion of many project writers when he said:

> "I got published and videotaped in a book! How cool is that?"

Students grow from authentic learning experiences and use them to formulate future goals. Authentic purposes make assignments meaningful for students. They help learners engage with the community and see value in their process. The community also benefits from the connection. Although it takes more work to coordinate, the benefits of authentic purpose are strong: student engagement and purposeful learning.

LISTEN AND BE KIND
Find a Love of Learning

I've said this before, but one of the only reasons I'm a writer is because I had a teacher in third grade who looked at my poem about clouds and said, 'You can be a writer when you grow up.' It stayed with me forever. Teachers, don't underestimate what your words can do for your students.
— CLINT SMITH III, WRITER AND AUTHOR

THE PROBLEM: Teachers have so much to do and can't make everyone happy

ALL TOO OFTEN, teachers feel burned out and underappreciated. We've all said and heard, "I have so many assignments to grade! Too many scores to enter!"

Teachers may also feel as if they are under a magnifying glass, with the constant pressures of lesson planning, taking attendance, relating to each student, grading, preparing students for college and the workforce, and delivering the curriculum.

During the pandemic, many of these pressures came into even greater focus. Teachers had more to consider: school shutdowns, teaching virtually, wearing masks, and quarantines. Many teachers seemed to question their value and the community's trust as contentious school board meetings surfaced on social media and political agendas were called into question. It seemed like the whole world watched and critiqued teachers—as well as student progression and learning loss. We heard, "Educators aren't doing enough" and "Kids are falling behind." The pressure, suffocating and immense, traumatized many teachers.

Department chairs, coordinators, leads, and superintendents gave teachers permission to let some things go, but teachers still lamented abandoning projects or cutting back on expectations or content.

Even without a pandemic, expectations seem to mount every year. Society is changing, and our school populations are morphing. Students come to our classrooms with more demands and needs. Teachers are asked to give and do more and more: sit on committees, advise extracurricular activities, earn professional development credits—plus teach concepts and strategies and prepare students for standardized testing and the workforce. We face all of these demands while our pay remains stagnant, making us feel underappreciated and taken for granted.

The ubiquitous technology in our classroom and in our students' hands makes many teachers feel dejected. Does anyone care that we're putting in extra hours or paying for supplies out of pocket? Does anyone listen? And when we reach out to the community or parents and guardians for support, we may not receive a positive response.

Students can feel this way too. They're moving through the day feeling rushed (do this now!), overwhelmed (here's your homework!), or despondent (here's your quiz grade!). A school day can leave everyone at the mercy of mandates and bells, and the love of learning and school gets lost under all that pressure.

THE HACK: Listen and be kind

Students do not require grading every day (or week or month). Each student is unique and requires different things at different times— but each student excels when met with a flexible, sensible approach.

Assessing the process allows you to differentiate for your students and to approach each student with kindness and empathy. There will be students who are unable to look you in the eye or students who remain combative and obstinate. But each student is on the verge of a breakthrough. Allow students to:

- build a sense of belonging and connection
- cultivate productive relationships
- feel positive about themselves and their progress
- enjoy the time they spend in your classroom
- believe in the power they have to respond to circumstances

YOU ARE MUCH MORE THAN A ROBOT GRADER OR QUIZ CORRECTOR. YOU ARE A PROFESSIONAL, DOING WHAT'S BEST FOR YOUR STUDENTS AS YOU HELP THEM CREATE LEARNING HABITS.

This approach also affords you humanity; you are much more than a robot grader or quiz corrector. You are a professional, doing what's best for your students as you help them create learning habits. Although you cannot control what your students do, you can control how you respond to each one: with acceptance and encouragement.

One of my students wrote me the following note after our time together:

> "When we first met in summer school, I was expecting to walk into the room with some cranky teacher who was upset that she had to stay at school for the summer to teach the kids who couldn't pass. But you were so nice. Right off the bat you were different from all the other teachers.

I was totally caught off-guard when you made your first comment on one of my documents. It was the first time I saw a comment on my work that wasn't a correction, it was a compliment. You were actually acknowledging that something was good. It seems like a minute detail, but just small compliments help a lot. I don't think most teachers know how much just being nice can help. After that, writing wasn't a task I had to complete, it was something I couldn't even stop. As soon as I started typing or writing with my pencil, I didn't even know when to end it. I just wanted to keep going until I ran out of space. Just being nice goes a long way for some people.

I couldn't believe how calm you were about Xander's poem. He showed me the poem before he read it out loud and I was just waiting for him to hear all the things wrong with it, but you somehow managed to compliment him on certain parts of the poem. I've never seen a teacher who was able to see the good in everything. That was insane to me. You made those few weeks of summer school really enjoyable and actually useful.

As the summer school went on, I managed to learn a lot about writing, but also a lot about myself. I learned I really liked writing, and it's something I want to pursue as a possible career thanks to your help and encouragement. I don't think any other teacher I've had would have actually motivated me like you did. While teachers have been nice, no one ever went out of their way like you did."

To help build an atmosphere of compassion, show students you care. Additionally, encourage students to compliment each other. In the music theater department, incoming students are paired with veterans in a big sibling/little sibling relationship. This is often done with dance troupes and sports teams. The older students, who usually have a driver's license, help the younger ones get to rehearsal on time. They coach their little sibs in how to prepare for an audition, what to sing, and how to handle disappointment if they don't get the role they want. During class, big siblings compliment their little sibs on things they noticed: being persistent in dance rehearsal, taking the lead in a vocal section, and showing expression in an acting scene. Directors say these pairings establish strong and lasting relationships. The care of the older students offers a safe space for young, intimidated, or frightened freshmen, and the examples set by the older students establish an expectation of kind and generous attitudes.

WHAT YOU CAN DO TOMORROW

Because enjoyment leads to practice, it will lead to progress. Aim to make each experience in your classroom an enjoyable one.

- **Welcome students.** Students are more likely to risk failure and work through the process if they feel safe, welcome, and valued. Greet students at the door by name. Add to the greeting something you appreciate about the student. What does each student contribute to the classroom that is uniquely their own? Build in time for students to greet each other.

   The next time you see your students, follow up. How did their dentist appointment go? Did they pass their driver's test? Did they resolve the fight with their sibling? Did they get the new toy they wanted? Remembering small details about students shows them you care.

One of my colleagues makes her seating chart using sticky notes—one for each kid. She writes brief comments about each student on their sticky note, so even when the seats change, she has quick access to silly little details about them (who likes Harry Styles or who is scared of needles). During the first five days of school, she asks icebreaker questions and students fill out electronic forms so they can play student trivia.

- **Intentionally shift language.** Delivery impacts how words are received. When your first word in response is "no," the message is often received negatively. It can come off harsher than you intended. A small shift gives your message the best chance at being heard. For example, instead of saying "no problem," consider "my pleasure." When you notice students saying, "I'm sorry," consider asking them to rephrase with "thank you." "Sorry, I can't think of anything" could become "Thank you for giving me time to explore what I'm interested in."

  Reinforce students' strengths instead of focusing on their deficits. Highlight all the areas that are right, or challenge yourself to identify three positives for every correction. Students don't want constant judgment and evaluation. Provide a safe and supportive classroom for students to explore their innate desire to learn, grow, and get better.

- **Celebrate each other.** Kindness and enthusiasm build investment and allow hard work to flourish. Give students a list of class members. Next to each name, ask students to write something positive.

Then, compile the lists so each student sees what was written about them. Although this takes time, collecting and curating the responses gives you quality control and the opportunity to weed out negative comments. Consider printing these sheets on decorative paper or framing the responses.

You could also create a word art image for each student. The same could be done for your colleagues or anyone in your school community.

Language arts teacher Carol Whitehaus ended her eighteenth year as a teacher, not knowing if she would make it to the next year in the profession. She said, "I fell apart so badly I had to take FMLA for my mental illness. But at the end of the year, I received a personalized [word art image] from one of the student groups. … The way these work is that the words that are typed in the most by students show up the biggest. I was so happy to see groovy there, since that's the highest compliment a kid can pay me as it's my favorite word. But more than that, I was so moved that resilience showed up big, for I definitely was not feeling resilient. I looked at this damn thing every day this summer to remind me of what kind of teacher and human I am even when I was feeling really dark. The good news is that it was a very healing summer, and I had a fantastic first day of my nineteenth year." See Image 9.1 for an example of a student-created word art image.

Image 9.1

- **Create an exchange.** Pair your students with younger or older students (either in your building, district, or in another state or country). An exchange encourages students to consider another person's perspective, display gratitude, and connect with people outside the classroom. Working in inter-grade groups provides both a purpose for the work and an opportunity for students to practice collaboration, listening, and kindness. Letter- or email-writing could also be used to cultivate gratitude and empathy.

- **Be kind to yourself.** You are doing good work. You are making a difference for your students. You are enough. If students, parents, or administrators are giving you a hard time, remember this may not be a reflection of you or your work. Still, if your mood isn't the best, move. Hop on your bike, take the dog for a walk, or practice yoga. Action gives you a chance to feel better.

A BLUEPRINT FOR FULL IMPLEMENTATION

A series of good experiences will keep your systems running. Stack positive onto positive; this momentum will carry students through challenging tasks. Encourage students to believe they can. Once they believe, they will.

Step 1: Spend time away from your curriculum to know who sits in front of you.

Pronounce their names correctly. Use their preferred pronouns. Start each class with an engaging or fun activity. Consider a warmup game, a riddle, or a piece of trivia. Find ways to bring your students together. Play music or project a compelling or entertaining photograph as students walk into the classroom. Build excitement for the learning that's about to occur. Help students to find joy in school.

ALLOW FOR MOVEMENT AND TRY OUT DIFFERENT WAYS TO CELEBRATE, BE GRATEFUL, AND BUILD A HAPPY TEAM ATMOSPHERE.

Step 2: Provide a daily goal.

Post this on the board, say it out loud, and write it in your learning management system. Help students find a tangible success that sets them up to demonstrate mastery or proficiency. Example: If all you do today is (insert task here), that's a class period well spent.

Step 3: Be realistic and balanced.

Accept that every day will not be a good day. Expect challenges and remember that the students who display emotional outbursts might be scared, frustrated, confused, sad, guilty, jealous, overwhelmed, or depressed. Psychologist Dr. Jody Carrington suggests, "Every time you think of calling a kid 'attention-seeking' this year, consider changing it to 'connection-seeking' and see how your perspective changes."

If a student displays connection-seeking behavior, engage them in a conversation. Look for the root of the behavior. Support social-emotional skills. Students need help developing and practicing positive habits and relationships. Remind them that they are learners who approach what happens with a constructive eye for revision and improvement. They are confident, capable, and strong.

Step 4: Practice soft skills.

Soft skills help build students' resilience. Empathy helps students realize they are not alone, and it reduces stress. When a classmate talks, remind students to give the speaker their attention (look at them, put away their phones). It shows they care and they think what the person says is important. What soft skills make your classroom more enjoyable for everyone?

Step 5: Instill a predictable routine of celebration.

Explain and celebrate efforts. Effort-based praise is more effective than achievement-based praise. Effort-praise helps each student understand their success and how they can use it to achieve their next goal.

In his book *Delivering Happiness*, author Tony Hsieh suggests happiness is the key to successful performances. To help your students create habits of learning, focus on infusing your classroom with happiness. Depending on your students' grade level, you may want to consider bringing in treats or having celebration days, passing out stickers, playing songs or dance performances, starting the day with a motivational quote or a joke, doing a whip-around where each student shares weekend plans, emailing each student's grown-up a positive note before the end of the first term, and asking students to share a shout-out to a classmate who made a difference for them.

Use a predictable structure for celebration. When students know the routine, they look forward to the breaks, and this creates a positive, collaborative environment. Consider playing a game at the beginning of class, playing games during a break (the same or a different game), and ending class with a reflection (verbal or otherwise). Allow for movement and try out different ways to celebrate, be grateful, and build a happy team atmosphere.

OVERCOMING PUSHBACK

We will be better practitioners, and our students will be more successful performers, if we provide room for positivity and enjoyment.

No matter what I do, some students are so negative. You can help the most resistant students know they are in a safe and welcoming place and that you care about them and their performance. Maybe this means spending time with a student processing and working through emotions. Maybe this means giving a student time to be curious, follow a passion, work collaboratively, or use effort to make the impossible possible.

Even though students look disengaged, unhappy, or distracted, don't give up. Keep being positive and believing in your students and yourself. Slowly, students will turn around. And even if they don't, they may surprise you in five or ten or twenty years with an email about how they met their best friend in your class, how your class led them to patent an invention, or how you gave them the confidence to start their own business.

I taught a group of boys one year who challenged everything I said. Because they were talented, they believed they knew more. They were condescending to the other students and uncooperative with me. Five years after they graduated, one of them came to the school. He asked to speak with me privately, and he apologized. "We were really jerks.

I'm sorry," he said. "I learned a lot then, and I've learned a lot since then." Even though you may not see the results of your efforts now, sometimes you will see the results later. Other times, you may never know. But you are making a difference. Your efforts matter.

Teaching is about content, not enjoyment. When students enjoy their work, they're more likely to invest in it, and that's what produces the biggest learning gains.

Nancy Jorgensen noticed a boy who had been hanging out with a group that was negatively influencing him. She invited him to join her music theater troupe. He had a great voice but hadn't been working at making the most of his talents. He spent a year in the group, made new friends, and received positive feedback on his accomplishments. At the end of the year, he told everyone that being a part of the performance troupe saved his life. He hinted at mental health issues and problems at home and with friends. A safe place, with appropriate expectations and positive reinforcement, made a difference in this boy's life. And he learned a lot along the way. This scenario, Jorgensen says, was repeated several times in her career.

THE HACK IN ACTION

The more grateful and empathetic students are, the more they feel connected to your classroom, their school, and their community. After studying a historical event, reading a novel, or hearing a guest speaker, students can consider how a person or character felt. Students can also practice empathy and gratitude through letters, emails, texts, or conversations.

I start out each semester with a lesson on email etiquette. After learning about the parts of a successful email, students send two gratitude emails. They write several drafts of the emails before sending, and they focus on inserting specific examples or evidence and utilizing proper email form.

Student Kayla Esslinger said, "I loved our gratitude emails because I was able to express my love to so many important people in my life while also learning proper email etiquette, which is a skill I will always need in life." See Appendix G for Esslinger's email to her parents, and Appendix H for a letter my sister wrote to me and which I share with my students every year as an example.

Later in the semester, I ask students to write essays about people who have made a positive difference in their lives. Students write about teachers, coaches, principals, school resource officers, guidance counselors, janitors, or lunch staff. See Images 9.2 and 9.3 for handwritten and emailed notes from my students.

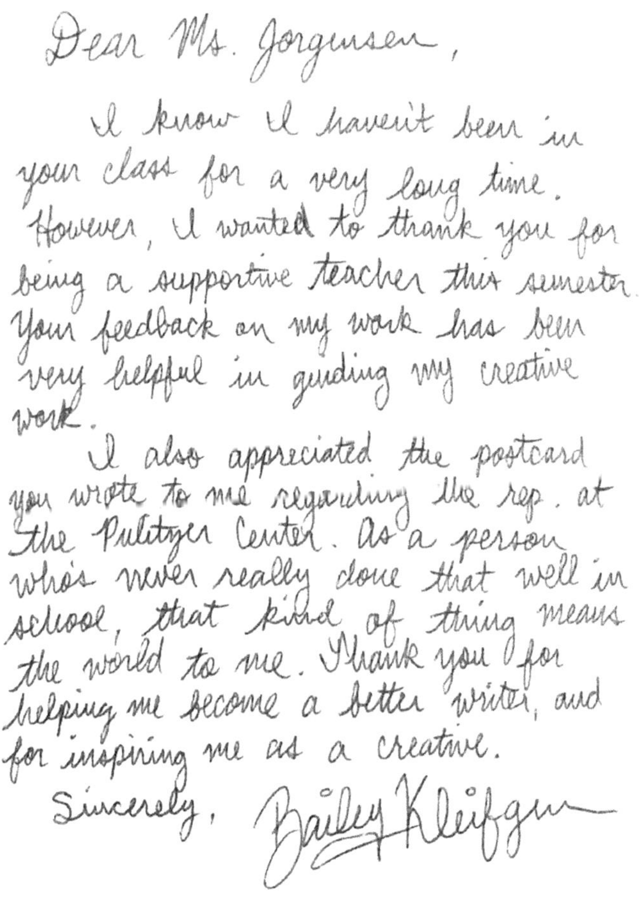

Dear Ms. Jorgensen,

I know I haven't been in your class for a very long time. However, I wanted to thank you for being a supportive teacher this semester. Your feedback on my work has been very helpful in guiding my creative work.

I also appreciated the postcard you wrote to me regarding the rep. at the Pulitzer Center. As a person who's never really done that well in school, that kind of thing means the world to me. Thank you for helping me become a better writer, and for inspiring me as a creative.

Sincerely, Bailey Kleifgen

Image 9.2

> ### Thank you for your class!
>
> Hello Mr. Jorgenson,
>
> I just wanted to let you know that I really loved your creative writing class and that one of the poems I wrote in your class got published! … I wanted to say thank you for encouraging me in my writing. After another English class this last semester I am taking another creative writing class this spring semester since I enjoyed your class so much. I hope that this finds you well and that you are inspiring more young writers to follow their passion.
>
> Sincerely,
> Luke Benson

Image 9.3

You can also write thank-you notes to your students. Emily Williams, an educator in Fort Worth, Texas, says, "I write my students thank-you notes all the time. I've noticed them re-reading the messages on difficult days, and sometimes they'll even write a response. It's precious."

The *Milwaukee Journal Sentinel* asked community members to "write and show your appreciation to a Wisconsin veteran [in the form of a letter] … All letters will be delivered to Stars and Stripes and will be distributed on future Honor Flights. For every letter received, the *Milwaukee Journal Sentinel* will make a $10 donation to the Stars and Stripes Honor Flight, up to $35,000." The *MJS* published one letter per week. See Image 9.4 for a collection of handwritten letters students created for veterans participating in an Honor Flight.

After my students wrote letters to veterans, they had this to say about the project:

"I have never thanked a veteran before, but I've always wanted to. I liked how personal this project gets. It was nice to be able to thank a veteran because it truly means something to them and if I could make a part of their day just a little bit better even, it's all worth it."

"I enjoyed this project because I think we often take what the veterans have gone through and done for us for granted. So I liked that we took time out of our day and had everyone thank them for their service."

"I liked the planning portion of the project so we got some ideas on what to include in our letter. I appreciate writing a letter to a veteran because I admire their bravery and sacrifices. It means a lot to them to get letters, even from people they don't know."

"I like that this project is something where we are recognizing and giving back to something outside of our sheltered worlds. I think this project is very meaningful and important. It gave me a chance to tell a veteran something other than 'thank you for your service.' It gave me a chance to direct my gratitude toward someone that truly deserves it."

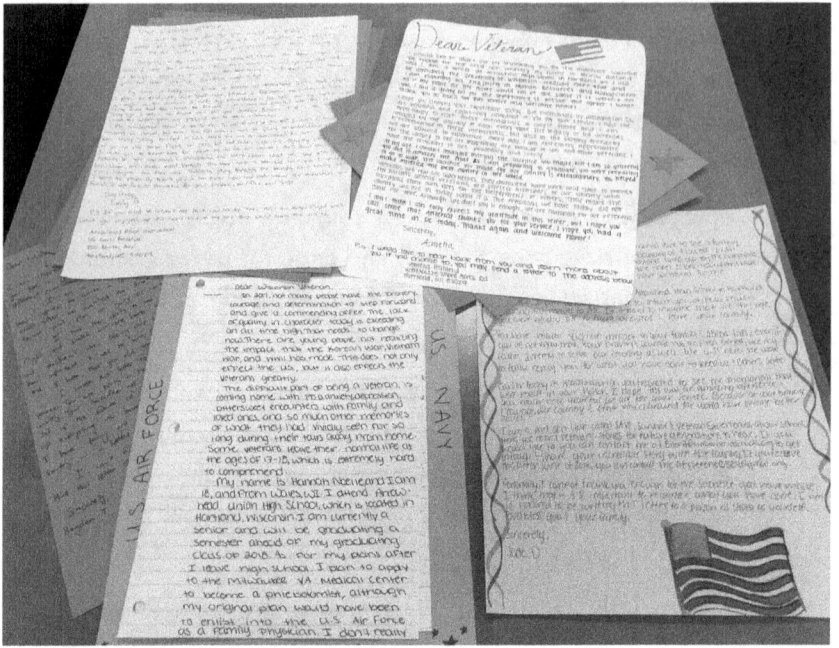

Image 9.4

●　●　●

Sometimes gratitude comes full circle years later. One day, after retiring from the field of education, Nancy Jorgensen stepped away from the mammogram imaging machine.

"Wait here," the technician said. "Stay in the hospital gown. I will let you know when the doctor has read your images." A few minutes later, the technician returned. "Don't be alarmed, but the doctor would like to speak with you." The technician handed the phone to Jorgensen.

"Hello. This is Nancy Jorgensen."

"Mrs. J! You were my choir director in high school, and I'm the doctor who is reading your mammogram." The former student went on to share how much she appreciated her experience in choir, described how she stays in touch with friends she met during choir, and said she still thinks about her choir trip to New York City.

Jorgensen and her student spent time reminiscing about the boy who insisted the group tour SoHo and another student who convinced Jorgensen to lead the group in a walk across the Brooklyn Bridge.

Of course, when Jorgensen taught choir, she didn't have to put in the extra effort to lead the New York City trip each year. The choir could have rehearsed and presented concerts without this traveling adventure. But she knew it was a hands-on learning experience, a much-anticipated break from daily rehearsals, and a reward for a year of hard work. While it was a valuable experience on its own, it was also a thank you to the students. Thank you comes in many forms. And fifteen years after Jorgensen showed students her appreciation, she received some in return.

Bring out the best in your students every day by meeting them where they are, listening, building trust, and coaching them to do more than they could before. When given a choice, choose optimism. This helps your students understand and receive your message. Find small ways to enhance your classroom. Ask students about their weekend plans. Wish them good luck at a meet or event. Send an email or postcard home.

How your students feel impacts their learning habits and processes. When you focus on where students are—both their strengths and their interests—students enjoy the process of lifelong learning.

INVEST IN, MAINTAIN, AND CELEBRATE THE PROCESS

'It is imperative that we support students in their iden-
tity as "learners" more than "knowers."
— CAREY BORKOSKI, EDUCATOR

TEACHERS TELL STUDENTS that in order to do well, they must read these pages, study these words, and memorize these terms. But what if our instructions send the wrong message? What if a blueprint to success does not exist? What if the steps we delineate don't work for all students? What if students don't enjoy the steps?

School often seems like a place of right or wrong answers, where only the correctly filled-in bubble is valued. Students analyze and solve for *the* answer, and this rigidity stalls enjoyment and growth. Students don't absorb and appreciate. They don't read a book to learn from it; they read to anticipate what will be on the quiz. They read thirty-five pages not to notice beautiful phrases or to appreciate nuance; they read pages because they were assigned. They cram. And nothing stays in their long-term memory. As soon as they take the test and leave the classroom, they forget the material. Students don't explore and experiment; instead, they memorize, regurgitate, and obliviate.

When teaching with a process-based assessment model, we give students:

- permission to be bad at something
- freedom to make mistakes
- guidance and support
- time, space, and grace to learn

Sometimes, forward movement seems hard—impossible, even. To keep moving forward, help students take a breath, stay in the moment, tackle items one at a time, and control the controllables. There are no shortcuts. There is only an accumulation of effort—a process of practice that compounds and allows consistency to outweigh magnitude.

INVITE STUDENTS TO BE FULLY PRESENT AND MINDFUL, TO TAKE CONTROL OF THEIR PROCESS RIGHT NOW.

Start by engineering an environment to make it easier for target behaviors to become habits, show students how to experience learning in ways they enjoy so they will look forward to it, and adopt a more flexible mindset while moving away from judgment. Give students both the structure and time to practice. This helps them explore creativity and passions.

Try to avoid polarizing viewpoints and opinions. If you present your process-based assessment model as an extreme change, you will meet more resistance and will be more likely to give up. You don't need a perfect plan. You need a balanced approach and continuing and compounding practice. A plan isn't about restriction but permission to try.

Empower students to focus on what they can do today. When encountering a roadblock, provide students with the time and room to regroup and refocus. Resist the urge to ask them to think about a week from now or a month from now—or to worry about the error that occurred yesterday or what could have been completed on Saturday. Instead, invite students to be fully present and mindful, to take control of their process right now.

Using their own interests and questions, students will deep-dive into a task. They aren't distracted by other classes, technology, or peers. They aren't thinking about what's right or wrong or what will be tested. They only consider what is doable right now, during this class. They are only focused on the present moment.

Most students just need someone to believe in them and genuinely care about them. Once they have this, they start to believe in themselves. As teachers, we need to help students unlearn what they've been taught about school. It's not about grades but about learning. Help students alter the way they think about school and focus on building healthy learning habits instead.

By assessing the process, you release achievement-driven pressure and give students responsibility over their choices. Students can do hard things. They can show up and practice, day after day. They can enjoy investments that yield results. They can be bad at something and then feel proud when they see growth.

Each student brings a different set of challenges, and you might feel like it's impossible to help all your students all the time, but know you're not alone. Every teacher has been there. Try to be as supportive of yourself as you are of your students. Take care of yourself. Build in time to read a book you enjoy or watch a movie with a loved one. Stick to your self-care routine, including exercise, nutrition, and adequate sleep. Maintain your positive, productive habits. Rely on your mantra to remember you are making a difference. You are helping so many students believe in themselves, grow, and love learning.

Utilize your support systems as needed. If a student situation is troublesome, reach out to a school resource officer, guidance counselor, department chair, or principal. Your colleagues can help delegate or provide resources for you and your students.

Your students have never done what you're asking them to do.

They are used to trying and giving up. They are used to failing and moving on without learning and growing. They need you to guide and support them, to encourage them to empower themselves to try and try again, to remind them of their strengths, and to help them manage their processes and make progress.

As you try out process-based assessment, be open to adjustments and new methods. Meet students where they are and support them as they reach for their full potential—and, most of all, find time to enjoy the process.

Believe in yourself. Trust the process. Change forever.
— BOB HARPER, PERSONAL TRAINER AND AUTHOR

APPENDIX A

A letter I provided to my students about process-based assessment at the beginning of the course:

Dear Student,

You are a young writer immersed in the messy process of sloughing off the stuff of childhood and, as the years advance, becoming more astute, more soulful, and more adult in your ability to communicate. To help you through the process, our course will emphasize improvement and growth.

This class will focus on skill development. You will learn new concepts and apply them to your pieces. Writing is not about being perfect. It is about practicing and improving.

You can expect to write daily and to complete multiple drafts. You can also expect to receive edits, suggestions, and corrections from both your peers and me.

Writing is a *process*, and your grade will reflect your daily work. And because you're expected to write daily, you will **not** be allowed to go back or submit late work. You will be provided ample time to complete and submit your assignment before the end of your class period. You will receive a process point if you complete the draft or task.

To become a better writer, you must work hard and accept constructive criticism. Please remember that critiques of your writing are not critiques of you. Proficient writing takes time to learn and even more time to apply. Every writer feels frustration, but (as with anything) it lessens with practice. Because composition is intended for sharing, you will read some of your work out loud and also send pieces to our school literary magazine and other writers' markets.

As an upperclassman, take ownership of your writing and progress. If you have questions or concerns, please do not hesitate to ask.

Your first assignment will be to reply to this letter. Please read the syllabus and then compose a response to me, summarizing and reacting to what you learned, posing questions, and setting goals for yourself. Tell me about your experience with writing and other English classes. State in your letter you understand process-based assessment and that no late work is accepted. Please also tell me what I need to know about you and your current situation.

I look forward to reading what you write.

Sincerely,

Ms. Jorgensen

APPENDIX B

A letter from a former student to a current student about process-based assessment:

Dear Future Composition Student:

I took Mrs. Carnell's Composition class my second semester junior year. There are many things that I enjoyed about the class—besides Mrs. Carnell herself—like the grading system. In Composition, every assignment is worth one point. Mrs. Carnell knows that everybody is in a different position in regards to their writing skills, so Mrs. Carnell doesn't care about how well you write, but your willingness to try and grow your abilities.

A day in Mrs. Carnell's class commences with pulling out your composition notebook. Mrs. Carnell will give you stylistic devices to write down and then a short prompt to write about to try and incorporate the new tactics you may have just learned. Mrs. Carnell loves when people are willing to share their work. In her class, there is no judgment and everything shared is greatly appreciated. It is important to read other people's works to not only help them but also yourself to grow your writing skills. Seeing something from another person's perspective is vital in writing.

Anaphora, allusion, anecdote. At the beginning of the semester, I didn't know what any of these meant, but now I am able to implement them in my writing. For example, I was able to use an anecdote (a short story that relates to a specific topic) to write an award-winning essay. To start my essay off, I began my story with "A small lanky six-year-old girl, her hair straight and brown held back by a feeble headband, sits among the chaos of a mess hall." With this, I framed my story. I was also able to use skills like metaphors and similes. For example, in an assignment about the meaning of my name, I used "My first name tastes like plain vanilla." I was able to use this as a recurring theme in my essay. With so many new skills, I have watched my writing grow. And with the help of Mrs. Carnell, I even got one of my pieces published.

Mrs. Carnell's class isn't about how well you can spell or how good your grammar is. In Mrs. Carnell's class, it is about your integrity and fortitude. And through every assignment, you are not working alone; she is always there to help and advise you. My advice to you: as you begin your journey into composition, be open to sharing your work with others. The benefits you will receive will amaze you. Good luck!

Sincerely,
A former student

APPENDIX C

Terri Carnell's pet peeve essay she provided as an example to her students:

"Please put your phones away," I say at the beginning of class. A simple request, I think, but unfortunately, it's not simple at all. It makes me sad—frustrated—enraged. My blood boils so intensely in my chest—symptoms of a heart attack.

Wonder. Worse than my poor, hurt pride, I wonder *Why? Why? Why? Am I so worthless as a human that no one cares what I say? Doesn't anyone care about anything anymore? Can't they hear me?* I have so many questions, and yet, I may never know the answers.

Concern. My desire to engage students is rooted in my concern for them. I genuinely want them to succeed not only in my class but in life. And so, this concern makes me fight.

Fight. I fight the battle every other day, nagging Billy to take his earbuds out. Reminding Sarah for the 91st time to please put her phone away. Asking Jamie to "stop playing pool."

"But I'm winning, Mrs. Carnell, just a minute," she says. And so I ask again … and again … and again.

Then they get creative. Texting from inside their pockets, saying, "My computer died, I need to type on my phone," or better yet, avoiding all eye contact—hoping that I may eventually give up or that I won't say anything about them using it right in front of me.

But, I'm a fighter. I ask them again to "Please, put your phones away," hoping that some ounce of humanity still exists in the depths of their souls, so they may LISTEN and finally PUT THEIR PHONES AWAY.

But then what? When the phones are in their backpacks, they get out their computers and have more distractions—Hudl, Netflix, TikTok.

And so I wait. And relax. And realize that maybe if I do require 9-1-1, I will be saved by one of the phones that was not put away.

APPENDIX D

An example of an email I sent to a parent and copied his two students:

Hello Jerry,

I hope you had a good weekend. I've CC'd both Connie and Sal on this email.

A little bit about Creative Writing: I view this class much like a choir or physical education or art class; students are asked to come in each day and practice and/or perform. In the syllabus and opening letter, I reviewed the assessment and grading policies; I also went over them verbally in class several times. Because writing is a process, and because I provide real-time feedback as they write, there is no going back and no late work is accepted. If Sal or Connie took another writing class (composition, for example), it's the same procedure (process-based assessment).

During class, I ask students to focus on the task at hand. Sal and Connie, even if you're not 100% confident with what you've done, hand *something* in. Please also make sure you're using the work time provided to focus on Creative Writing.

If you are stuck or don't know what to do, just ask! I am always here to assist! I hope this helps clarify.

Have a good day,
Ms. Jorgensen

APPENDIX E

An example of a positive email I sent to the parent of a student who volunteered to read her poem out loud to the class:

Dear Kathy,

I just wanted to drop you a quick note and let you know that Kami volunteered to present her poem in class today. Currently, students are working on a food-themed poem for the Milwaukee Public Museum's annual poetry competition.

After we read Kami's poem, classmates provided valuable feedback and encouragement. If you are interested, I would suggest you ask her to share what she is working on. I think you'll be impressed!

Volunteering to read her poem to the class was a brave, vulnerable, and commendable thing to do! Please encourage Kami to keep up the great work in Creative Writing.

I'm looking forward to a wonderful semester of writing, creativity, and growth!

Liz :)

APPENDIX F

I AM UNIQUE
by Dalton Hribar

I am not the one who will blame others,
I am not one to fight with brothers.
I am not the one who sits doing nothing,
I am not the one who will call something disgusting.
I am not the car which stands idle,
I am not the one who has a rival.
I am not the one who has enemies,
I am not the one who dismisses extremities.
I am not one who divides,
I am not the one who has too much pride.
I am not the one who is quiet,
I am not the one who strays from the dict.
I am not the one who takes things for granted,
I am not the bad bandit.

I am not the calm sea,
I am not the one to spill the tea.
I am not the weak voice,
I am not the one to make the wrong choice.
I am not one who focuses on the past,
I am not the one to outcast.
I am not the one who lacks faith,
I am not the one to be in eighth.
I am not the one to follow the social norm,

I am not one to stay uniform.
I am not the rainy day,
I am not the one to go astray.

I am not the darkness in the night,
I am not the one who has no might.
I am not the one who cuts the trees,
I am not the one who doesn't feel the breeze.
I am not the fire that lays dormant,
I am not the one who disobeys enforcement.
I am not the einstein,
I am not the flat wine.
I am not a number,
I am not a humbugger.
I am not red,
I am not misled.
I am not the skier,
I am not the one to fear.
I am not the one to be alone,
I am not a cyclone.
I am unique!

APPENDIX G

An email message that student Kayla Esslinger wrote to her parents as part of a gratitude and email etiquette project:

Dear Mom and Dad,

I hope your day is off to a great start! I know I will see you both later tonight, but I just wanted to write this email to express my gratitude towards both of you. For 17 years now, you have raised me and made me into the person I am today. I love and appreciate you guys so much and I don't know how I would get by without you. I always feel like I don't express just how much I love you, and I really should because my heart is overflowing with love for both of you.

Mom—I love going on car rides together, blasting the music and laughing until we're both about to pee our pants. I love sitting by the fire in the sunroom together and talking about our days.

Dad—I love relaxing in the sunroom together while eating custard and laughing about Lucy. I love hearing the door open when you get home from work because I know that my forever super hero is home.

As a family—I love our walks together as we toss the football and watch the sunset. I love having dinner together and knowing how much love we all share. I love you. I hope you both have an amazing day because you deserve it. Can't wait to see you when I get home!

With love,
Kayla

APPENDIX H

This is a treasured letter that my sister, Gwen Jorgensen, posted to me in honor of International Women's Day and Women's History Month. I share it with my students as an example of a thoughtful letter.

Dear Elizabeth,

When I was five years old I wanted to do everything you did. You were my peer, mentor, best friend. I played the violin because that's what you played. I joined the basketball team because I saw you shooting hoops. Showed up at track camp because you were enrolled too.

As I grew up I became my own person, no longer dribbling a basketball behind you, but observations continued. You started playing more instruments and excelling in language arts. I was exploring my own sport while learning math equations.

As a child I was most thankful for you talking for me, and sometimes I still wish you were with me to answer questions for me. Instead, you make phone calls I don't want to make, help me write sponsorship letters, fix up my house, and have the best ideas of what to eat or where to go. But what I appreciate most is your unconditional support. No matter what I choose to do, you show up. Thank you for decorating cars, making tshirts, and traveling anywhere and everywhere to cheer me on. It's my dream to live next door to you, but until that can happen I hope to continue to make memories at photo shoots in CA, Olympic Houses, and Airbnbs around the world.

You are passionate, caring, and make my life better. I can't imagine life without you, Sister. It's Women's History Month, and this is the perfect time to thank you. You are the one who taught me to be a strong woman. That I can do anything I want. To not care about what others say, think, or do. You taught me to support myself through your example of becoming an RA to pay your own tuition. You showed me that I too can create my own path. By mimicking your every move, I learned to create my own life.

You're the one who taught me about track and field. Without you I never would have run. Thank you for giving me the joy of running, it's changed my life in ways I never could have imagined.

Love,
GW

ABOUT THE AUTHOR

Elizabeth Jorgensen is an award-winning writer and teacher and sought-after speaker. In 2021, she was named one of the twenty America's Most Inspiring Educators (The Henry Ford's Innovation Nation Teacher Innovator Awards).

She has been published in *English Journal, Edutopia, Teachers & Writers Magazine, Azalea: Journal of Korean Literature and Culture* (Harvard University), *Brevity, Milwaukee Journal Sentinel, Writers Who Care, Ohio Journal of English Language Arts, Wisconsin English Journal, Skinny Poetry Journal*, and *Gyroscope Review*, among others.

She has presented for the National Council of Teachers of English, Wisconsin State Reading Association, Wisconsin Writers Association, East Asian Studies Center at Indiana University, The Ohio Council of Teachers of English Language Arts, and The Illinois Reading Council, among others.

Jorgensen is passionate about sijo, a Korean form of poetry. Her sijo lessons have been uploaded by the Sejong Cultural Society as an exemplar of teaching poetry, and she was a runner-up in the 2020 Wisconsin Sijo Contest.

Her memoir was published in 2019. Narrated in alternating voices, *Go, Gwen, Go: A Family's Journey to Olympic Gold* (Meyer & Meyer Sport) is an inspiring story about Olympian Gwen Jorgensen and her family.

Hundreds of Elizabeth's students have been published or won writing awards.

In 2017, Jorgensen was named the Graduate of the Last Decade from Carroll University. For the 2014-2015 school year, Jorgensen was named the Arrowhead Union High School (Hartland, Wisconsin) Teacher of the Year.

She received her undergraduate degree from Marquette University (Milwaukee, Wisconsin) and her master's from Carroll University (Waukesha, Wisconsin). Visit her website, lizjorgensen.weebly.com.

ACKNOWLEDGMENTS

THANK YOU ...

To Mark Barnes, for knowing I had this book in me and for inviting me to join the Hack Learning Series. I am grateful you believed in me and my vision of education.

To Jennifer Jas, my amazing editor. Thank you for being my source of endless optimism and guidance. And thank you to the entire Times 10 Publications team for helping me bring this book to life.

To my writing teacher colleagues, Terri Carnell, Heidi Hamilton, and Rebecca McCann. Thank you for fearlessly exploring process-based assessment with me, for working through messy and scary changes, and for being the teachers I would have loved in high school.

To my administration, including Sue Casetta, Dave Gierach, Laura Myrah, and Gregg Wieczorek. We could not have implemented process-based assessment without you. Thank you also to the Wisconsin Department of Instruction and the Every Teacher a Leader Summit.

To the teachers who shared their classrooms and students with me. You illuminated the different ways educators are using process-based assessment to engage students.

To Rick Witte, who spent hours asking me questions. You were instrumental in helping me clarify my jumbled thoughts into nine Hacks.

To my family, who checked in on me, encouraged me, believed in me, and read early drafts. You were essential to my process.

To all of the educators who hack learning: thank you for welcoming me to the Times 10 Publications authors' club.

To my beta readers, Terri Carnell and Nancy Jorgensen. I am so grateful to work alongside each of you. You are true role models.

To my sister, who helped me realize all I had to do was be average every day.

To my mom and my writing partner. Your books, *Things They Never Taught You in Choral Methods* and *From the Trenches: Real Insights from Real Choral Educators*, paved the way for my dreams and this book.

To my dad, my cheerleader. Thank you for your unending support and help, especially when it comes to building and fixing.

To Josh, for knowing when I need a break and for impromptu date nights. I love you as much as you love Casper.

To all of my students who trusted me with words and stories. I am humbled by the process we built together. Thank you.

MORE FROM
TIMES 10 PUBLICATIONS

Browse all titles at 10Publications.com

Hacking School Discipline
9 Ways to Create a Culture of Empathy & Responsibility Using Restorative Justice
By Nathan Maynard and Brad Weinstein

Reviewers proclaim this *Washington Post* Bestseller to be "maybe the most important book a teacher can read, a must for all educators, fabulous, a game changer!" Teachers and presenters Nathan Maynard and Brad Weinstein demonstrate how to eliminate punishment and build a culture of responsible students and independent learners in a book that will become your new blueprint for school discipline. Eighteen straight months at #1 on Amazon and still going strong, *Hacking School Discipline* is disrupting education like nothing we've seen in decades—maybe centuries.

Hacking Modern Teaching
10 Ways to Build Student Engagement, Maximize Success, and Inspire Authentic Learning
By Mike Roberts

Modern teaching is not about your ability to deploy a flashy education app; it's a mindset where you keep student success at the forefront of your instruction. Today's teachers have a unique opportunity to reflect on their values, rethink their lessons, and reevaluate what is essential to meet the needs of modern students. In *Hacking Modern Teaching*, Mike Roberts offers modern teaching hacks to help today's teachers maximize student engagement and success.

Browse all titles at 10Publications.com

Hacking Assessment
10 Ways To Go Gradeless In a Traditional Grades School
By Starr Sackstein

Award-winning teacher and world-renowned formative assessment expert Starr Sackstein unravels one of education's oldest mysteries: how to assess learning without grades—even in a school that uses numbers, letters, GPAs, and report cards. Teachers like Sackstein are reimagining education. This book shows you exactly how to create a vibrant no-grades classroom where students grow, share, thrive, and become independent learners who never ask, "What's this worth?"

Teaching in Magenta
100 Paths to Joy and Well-being for You and Your Students
By James Alan Sturtevant; Illustrated by Lauren Barnes

What does it mean to teach in magenta? Magenta is bold, it's vibrant, and it holds noble qualities. *Teaching in Magenta* means creating magnificent days. It's a refreshing approach to teaching that puts your joy and well-being first so you can share those attributes with students. Veteran teacher and author James Sturtevant shares one hundred paths for living and teaching in an authentic, enthusiastic, and relevant way. Find renewed joy in teaching and become a refreshingly magenta teacher.

Browse all titles at 10Publications.com

Hacking Flex Teaching
10 Solutions for Your Blended, Hybrid, or Distance Learning Classroom
By Hollie Woodard

Education and technology have merged, forever changing the way students learn. Teachers need guidance in this flexible world of education technology to create one lesson format that streamlines teaching, engages students, and elevates learning outcomes. In *Hacking Flex Teaching*, author Hollie Woodard offers solutions and best practices that apply to all virtual classrooms. She helps teachers strategize their planning by choosing the least amount of work, in the least amount of time, for the best possible learning outcomes.

Hacking Learning Centers in Grades 6–12
How to Design Small-Group Instruction to Foster Active Learning, Shared Leadership, and Student Accountability
By Starr Sackstein and Karen Terwilliger

Learning centers are dynamic spaces where students can become robust thinkers, problem-solvers, and brave leaders. *Hacking Learning Centers in Grades 6–12* shares *why* and *how* to design small-group instruction that includes everyone and encourages students to collaborate, experiment, reflect, self-assess, and transfer the learning to their lives beyond school. Starr Sackstein and Karen Terwilliger show how learning centers empower unexpected leaders, raise the bar on student accountability, activate the fun to bring learning to life, and inspire students to share ideas and make decisions.

Browse all titles at 10Publications.com

RESOURCES FROM TIMES 10 PUBLICATIONS

Nurture your inner educator:
10publications.com/educatortype

Podcasts:
hacklearningpodcast.com
jamesalansturtevant.com/podcast

On Twitter:
@10Publications
@HackMyLearning
#Times10News
#RealPBL
@LeadForward2
#LeadForward
#HackLearning
#HackingLeadership
#MakeWriting
#HackingQs
#HackingSchoolDiscipline
#LeadWithGrace
#QuietKidsCount
#ModernMentor
#AnxiousBook
#HackYourLibrary

All things Times 10:
10Publications.com

TIMES 10 PUBLICATIONS provides practical solutions that busy educators can read today and use tomorrow. We bring you content from experienced teachers and leaders, and we share it through books, podcasts, webinars, articles, events, and ongoing conversations on social media. Our books and materials help turn practice into action. Stay in touch with us at 10Publications.com and follow our updates on Twitter @10Publications and #Times10News.

.

www.ingramcontent.com/pod-product-compliance
Lightning Source LLC
Chambersburg PA
CBHW061151120626
46546CB00005B/2011